THE POLISHED KING

Living Words of Martin Luther King Jr.

JOSEPH EVANS

Foreword by Marvin A. McMickle

The Polished King

Interior design by Wendy Ronga, Hampton Design Group.
Cover design by Danny Ellison.

Library of Congress Cataloging-in-Publication data
Names: Evans, Joseph (Dean of Morehouse University School of Religion), author. Title: The polished King: living words of Martin Luther King, Jr. / Joseph Evans. Description: Valley Forge, PA: Judson Press, 2021. | Includes bibliographical references and index. Identifiers: LCCN 2021038074 (print) | LCCN 2021038075 (ebook) | ISBN 9780817018337 (paperback) | ISBN 9780817082376 (epub) Subjects: LCSH: King, Martin Luther, Jr., 1929-1968—Language. | King, Martin Luther, Jr., 1929-1968—Oratory. | Baldwin, James, 1924-1987—Language. | English language—United States—Rhetoric. | Speeches, addresses, etc., American—History and criticism. Classification: LCC E185.97.K5 E93 2021 (print) | LCC E185.97.K5 (ebook) | DDC 323.092 [B]—dc23
LC record available at https://lccn.loc.gov/2021038074
LC ebook record available at https://lccn.loc.gov/2021038075

Printed in the U.S.A.
First printing, 2021.

To Matthew Zacharias Evans,
my only son, whom I unconditionally love.
"Take the point."
John 14:6

CONTENTS

Foreword

I have been collecting, reading, and passing on books both by and about Martin Luther King, Jr. even before his assassination in 1968. I have three shelves in my study devoted entirely to these books. Some of these books take a historical look at the life of Dr. King. The three volumes produced by Taylor Branch fit into that category. The books by Lerone Bennett, Jr., Clarence Jones, Lewis Baldwin, C. Eric Lincoln, and David Levering Lewis take us inside the life and even the prayers and private thoughts of King. Collections of King's writings—such as the exhaustive volume compiled by James Melvin Washington and the equally essential collection of sermons edited by Clayborne Carson and Peter Holloran—take us back to the speeches, essays, interviews, and sermons that propelled King to international fame and to the Nobel Peace Prize awarded to him in 1964. One of the most recent attempts to examine the words and work of King is *The Sword and the Shield* by Peniel Joseph that compares and contrasts the lives of King and Malcolm X.

There are the books written by King himself between 1956 and 1967. These books include *Stride Toward Freedom*, *Why We Can't Wait*, *Strength to Love*, *The Measure of a Man*, *The Trumpet of Conscience*, and *Where Do We Go from Here: Chaos or Community*. If someone has the audacity to bring forth another book about Martin Luther King, Jr. considering all that has already been written about him and by him, that book better be good. It better bring a fresh angle from which the words and work of King can be viewed.

What is left to be said? What more can be uncovered or revealed that the last fifty-plus years of scholarship has not already produced? Then a new book does emerge that offers us something new. It is *The Polished King* by Joseph Evans with a great assist from the novelist, James Baldwin. It was James Baldwin who coined the phrase "a polished preacher." It is Evans who takes us behind that phrase and reveals the people and practices within the black Baptist church and within black communities across the United States, whose guiding hand and cultural norms helped shape, mold, and polish King into the person he eventually became.

Dr. King did not emerge onto the American scene out of nowhere. He came from a very specific somewhere. He came from Ebenezer Baptist Church in Atlanta, Georgia, and from Auburn Avenue in Atlanta in the 1930s and 1940s, where the Sunday morning music of the church and the Saturday night rhythms of the community created a culture that nurtured and nourished the heart and mind of a young Martin Luther King, Jr. King came from his grandfather, A.D. Williams and his father, Martin Luther King, Sr. He also came from a church and a home where the best of black leadership was frequently present as a reminder that there was more to life than Auburn Avenue. The first coat of polish was applied at home.

The second coat of polish was applied at Morehouse College, where the guiding hand of its President, Dr. Benjamin Elijah Mays, and the monumental influence of one of the alumni of Morehouse College—namely Howard Thurman—challenged King to rethink his theology and reimagine his reason for living. King was becoming a model of the black Baptist preacher that was different from what was the norm in most such churches in the 1940s and early 1950s. For King, preaching required more that emotionalism and lung capacity. It required more than five minutes of content and fifteen minutes of whooping. King was developing a style that was as cerebral as it was emotional, as thoughtful and provocative as it was rhythmic and cadenced.

The Polished King was touched by other hands and models of ministry. There was Samuel Dewitt Proctor, who preceded him at both Crozer Theological Seminary and at Boston University. There was Gardner Calvin Taylor, whom King first encountered at the National Baptist Convention USA, Inc., and who would later become instrumental in the formation of the Progressive National Baptist Convention, Inc., that provided King with a national, church-based program from which to operate. I know something about this layer of polish, since both men were central to my own ministry development. Of course, hundreds of others could and gladly do make the same claim! The idea of The Polished King reminds me of what someone said about William Augustus Jones, Jr. after he had presided over an annual session of the Progressive National Baptist Convention: "That man has been rubbed awhile." Jones was another polished preacher.

The key insight of Joseph Evans in this book is what that polishing produced in King's preaching and speaking style. Being world-class in the fields of homiletics and rhetoric, Evans picked up the unique use of language employed by Martin Luther King, Jr. More precisely, Evans points to King's use of metaphor, of living words that had the power to transform the world into which they were spoken. Evans borrows a phrase from Eddie Glaude, Jr. of Princeton University who said, "Dr. King moved the nation with the soul of the black church…as a preacher moves a congregation." "I Have a Dream." "I've Been to the Mountaintop." "An island of poverty surrounded by a great sea of material prosperity." These phrases were not just parts of famous speeches delivered by King. They were metaphors—living words—the use of language that created memorable images that were implanted into the hearts of King's listeners.

The discussion about metaphor in *The Polished King* brings to mind one of King's closest allies, Rabbi Abraham Joshua Heschel. In a collection of his writings, his daughter, Susanna Heschel states that her father often said, "words can make worlds."[1] Whether for good or for evil, words have the power to shape the world into which those words are spoken. Heschel noted that Hitler's words came before any of his hateful actions that resulted in the Holocaust. Similarly, King's words came first, and those words helped produce the world that gave us the 1964 Civil Rights Bill and the 1965 Voting Rights Act.

Evans refers to this use of metaphor and living words by yet another set of terms, *transformative and transformational words.* Those words were not limited solely to the issue of racial reconciliation, as many white conservative pundits would prefer, freezing King into a single moment in time and a single phrase about being judged by the content of one's character and not just the color of one's skin. Evans reminds us that King's transformational and transformative words reached into the issues of poverty and economic inequity, unfair labor practices, and the way the war in Viet Nam wasted human lives and national resources. I have never heard Tucker Carlson or Sen.Josh Hawley quote from those words by Dr. King!

Evans points to one example of the use of metaphor that readers should consider. He talks about the first time King was forced to sit behind a curtain on a railroad dining car that separated white and black passengers. In discussing that experience, King draws a larger meaning from that moment. King says, "I felt as if the curtain had been dropped on my selfhood." Thus, the curtain on the railroad car was not just about the rules of segregation that had existed in parts of this country since *Plessy v. Ferguson* established the so-called "separate but equal" provision in all areas of public life in 1896.

Martin Luther King, Jr. did not create this use of metaphor. He was, as Evans argues, "among the inheritors of the black preaching tradition." At another point, Evans states that King was "a legatee of a great preaching tradition." That black preaching tradition played a key role in shaping the Polished King.

Martin Luther King, Jr. was shaped by the demands of the Montgomery Improvement Association in the year-long bus boycott that followed the arrest of Rosa Parks in 1955 for failing to give up her seat "in the colored section" to a white male who wanted her to stand so he could sit. It was here where Dr. King began to outgrow the narrow limits then associated with being the pastor of a local congregation. Following the example of Vernon Johns, his predecessor at Dexter Avenue Baptist Church in Montgomery, Alabama, King felt the call to confront and openly condemn the racism, segregation, and physical intimidation perpetrated by white people against black people every day in this country. There were death threats against him and his family. His home in Montgomery was bombed while his wife Coretta and first-born child Yolanda were inside. There is no way to understand Martin Luther King, Jr. without traveling with him during that formative year from 1955 to 1956. That was part of the polishing process that prepared him for the trials that would lie ahead.

What goes on in the mind of a man who knows that he will not live to see his fortieth birthday? How do you spend your time? How do you choose your battles? How do you overcome your fears when you know that every day could be your last, not because of any physical ailments that might attack your body, but because of the sickness of racism and racialized violence that has infected this country since 1619? With my own eyes, I saw Dr. King lead marches and confront tyrants and suffer physical assault and move into spaces where an assassin's bullet could have struck him down long before James Earl Ray did so in Memphis in 1968. Facing life with courage and conviction requires a special kind of person. That was the person James Baldwin encountered. That was the man he called "a polished preacher." That was the *Polished King* that Joseph Evans has helpfully and skillfully set before us in this timely new book.

Manuel Scott, Sr. —another polished black preacher whose ministry touched every corner of this country and every national convention, both black and white—is reported to have said: "It takes a lot of people to make a preacher." In my book, *The Making of a Preacher*, I echo the sentiments of Manuel Scott when I assert that "Preachers are not born, they are made."

> *Preachers are made by stages of development over time. Preachers are made as they search for their own authentic voice and style, freeing themselves from becoming clones of the persons who have had the most influence on their lives and their ministry. Preachers are made when they learn how to preach within the context of their own time and place in history."*[2]

The Polished King concludes with Evans paying close attention to the preaching/teaching style of Jesus, especially in his use of parable, which are metaphors and living words. We get a careful review of how King made use of biblical parables to organize his sermons and communicate his message. It should come as no surprise that it was Jesus Christ who applied the final coat of polish to the heart and mind, to the words and work, to Martin Luther King, Jr., the man James Baldwin called "a polished preacher."

Notes

1. Tana M. Schiewer, *Words Create Worlds: Alternative Worlds and the Words That Dismantle Them*, medium.com, February 7, 2017.
2. Marvin A. McMickle, *The Making of a Preacher: 5 Essentials for Ministers Today* (Valley Forge, PA: Judson Press, 2018).

CHAPTER 1

In Search of a Polished Preacher

> I first met Martin Luther King, Jr., nearly three years ago now, in Atlanta, Georgia. He was there on a visit from his home in Montgomery [Alabama]. He was "holed up," he was seeing no one, he was busy writing a book—so I was informed by a friend, who mercilessly, at my request, was taking me to King's hotel.
> —James Baldwin[1]

Preachers in the Black church tradition are called to preach. Therefore, if we can preach, we are divinely called and obligated to pursue the church's expectation, which is to become recognized as polished preachers. James Baldwin's quest for truth prompted him to affirm after his impromptu meeting with Martin Luther King Jr. that King was indeed a polished preacher. My commitment in this book is to reinforce that King is a quintessential polished preacher.

Countless volumes about King have been published, including many biographies that contribute to our understanding of his social ethics.[2] Still others emphasize his political and economic context. That context influenced the shape and content of many socio-histories in the 1950s and '60s. Other books on library shelves are concerned with King's leadership style, a style that defines the nation's most significant human rights struggle: the civil rights era and movement.

Nevertheless, there is room and need for another King volume. The purpose of this volume is to remind readers that King, an ordained Baptist preacher, was rooted in the Black church tradition. My intent is to emphasize that Baldwin recognized King as a polished preacher. I point toward King's traits, attributes, and yes, his gifts. I suggest that above all else, Baldwin was attracted to King's living words, for it is a polished preacher's words that attract people toward her or his movement. Martin Luther King mastered living words. His rhetoric is a work of art; his words demand that action be taken.

My thesis is simple: King is a polished preacher because he employs living words that represent symbols which together make people aware of Divinity's transcending presence and power made manifest and recognized as the emergent kingdom of God.[3] I further suggest that King's living words are metaphors that open windows that shed light on his theology.[4] I contend that King's theology is metaphoric and perhaps a forerunner of postmodern theology.[5] King's theology is formed and shaped by a species of rhetoric. In short, King's narrative, rhetoric, theology, and homiletic intersect.

James Baldwin Meets a Polished Preacher

Baldwin was a gifted writer and a provocative thinker, and his prophetic honesty underscores his life and transparent literature. Baldwin's truth telling emerges through his published writings and public addresses. His short, sincere dialogue is intended to abolish discrimination in all forms. Like King's, Baldwin's literature makes visible something I call hegemonic human constructs, or what one scholar calls "the lie."[6] What is more, any fair reading of Baldwin's literature, readers will agree, points toward human dysfunctions and uncovers our fault lines. If we are to understand Baldwin's writings as literature, we must take seriously his honesty and commitment to bring truth to light.

Baldwin's initial meeting with King was filled with anxieties. But Baldwin discovered that King was not pretentious: "Reverend King is not like any preacher that I have ever met before. For one thing, to state it baldly, I liked him." Baldwin continued, "I felt terribly guilty about interrupting him but not guilty enough to let the opportunity pass. Still, having been raised among preachers, I would not have been surprised if King had cursed out the friend, refused to speak to me, and slammed the door in our faces. Nor would I have blamed him if he had, since I knew that by this time, he must have been forced to suffer many an admiring fool."[7]

Baldwin's remarks demonstrate his honest transparency. He does not leave us to speculate cravenly about his inner feelings concerning King: "It is rare that one likes a world-famous man—by the time they become famous they rarely like themselves, which may account for his antipathy."[8] By this I take Baldwin to mean that King was disliked because of envy and jealousy based on perceptions of King's privilege, which upset many whites and some Blacks.

Baldwin may have been describing in an adroit fashion his own cost; he paid for fame. It is subtle, but we hear his own struggles, perhaps his internal fight against his self-dislike and personal antipathy. Some were envious about Baldwin's emerging success as a writer, and others were jealous of his prophetic voice inside the Black community. Like W. E. B. Du Bois, Baldwin sought to lift the veil from Eurocentrism.

What is more daunting, Baldwin may have exposed his own guarded sense of hope about the future. When King or Baldwin and others like them stand against dominating forces, they may feel coldly disguised indifference from their adversaries. Here, I think, Baldwin transferred his inner hope about the future, which masqueraded as dread, to King. Whatever the case, Baldwin was prophetic and foresaw and forecast King's fateful future.[9]

King's fame was not something he sought or hoped for, and his fame was something to dread because it was thrust upon him by his dogged hope in divinity and people. A thin line exists between faith and fate, hope and dread. Still, Baldwin confirmed, King was different from other preachers. Many others had disappointed him, for Baldwin wanted more from Black preachers.[10] He wanted to witness their courage to face complexities of evil outside the doors of storefronts and cathedrals.[11] King was that kind of preacher—the kind Baldwin longed to witness.

King, then, provided for Baldwin a sense of trust in his own hope masquerading as dread. Described still another way, King offered Baldwin space to trust his own pessimistic optimism. Long before meeting King, Baldwin had idealized what he believed to be a polished preacher as one who handles Divine oracles and possesses capacities to interpret and make plain oracles that remain clouded. A polished preacher is a responsible steward over such dimly lit oracles (Divinity's revelation). If a polished preacher is clear, people are able to make informed judgments.

For those who accept their responsibility to make judgments about truth claims, their task is easier if a polished preacher is recognized as a person who is gifted with an oracle's insight. In addition, a polished preacher comes equipped with confidence to stand as an authenticated proclaimer of Divinity's transcendent presence and power.[12] It is Divinity's existence, moral and ethical righteousness, that indwells a polished preacher and affirms hope to people.[13] This is what defines a polished preacher.

Through a polished preacher's words that represent symbols, Divinity's existence comes into the world. That is, words and symbols awaken us and provide possibilities that we associate with Divinity. King's words represent symbols that confirm the purpose of the Divine, which is to change the course of fatal human behavior toward the creation. For, we must admit, people contribute to inhumane and toxic environments. In short, King's words and symbols associated with transcendent divine presence, power, existence, and possibilities give a polished preacher courage to declare truth claims, and these declarations vitalize human frailness.

A polished preacher has mastery over the currency of words and symbols. King used this life-giving ability to inspire human courage to pursue democratic justice. Let us attempt to be as honest and transparent as Baldwin. We know that King was misunderstood by many, and that fact was and is a challenge. The greater challenge then and now, however, is people who did understand King, namely, his opponents. Although his opponents understood his commitments to democratic principles and justice, his opponents could not accept that King's deep commitments to democracy and justice are ethical mandates that point toward King's love of all people. In short, Baldwin grasped that King represented what he longed to witness—his polished preacher. On one hand, polished preachers are people who take on challenges larger than any of us, not foreseeing where a cause will take them. On the other hand, polished preachers may know exactly what they face. In King's case, he knew he faced racial hatred from the masses, but he also faced racism from what I characterize as nearly invisible opponents. King's living words, however, pulled invisible opponents out of obscurity.

To confront and abolish racism and other forms of discrimination, a polished preacher understands that invisible opponents spin webs of oppression and discerns how their webs are connected. These webs have guardians whose primary role is to guard the status quo (these point toward the nation's institutional spheres). A polished preacher like King is called to disrupt the status quo by using words that represent symbols that point to the realities of these spun webs.[14] Once these webs are revealed, a polished preacher like King must develop strategies to make plain that these webs are destructive and therefore must be deconstructed to abolish them. King employed words that represent symbols to confront visible and invisible adversaries' immoral and unethical webs that entangle people in destructive behaviors.[15]

Baldwin inferred as much. For King and other polished preachers, Divinity must indwell them and gift each with unfounded courage to face foreseeable and unforeseeable uncertainties. Seldom does Divinity disclose a full blueprint to a polished preacher. Frequently, a polished preacher is given merely sketches. King may be regarded as an architect of the most notable socio-human movement in American history, but he worked primarily from sketches.

Still, King was the epitome of baptism in the name of Jesus that results in the gift of the Holy Spirit (Acts 2:38-39). This is an example of what Baldwin envisioned, the personification of a polished preacher. Even more, King embodied an instinctive fluidity and feel for words and symbols. That is, polished preachers are endowed with an unlimited currency of words and symbols, much as Baldwin was endowed. For a polished preacher, words as symbols come as an issued tool kit, the kind with directions printed on the outside of the box. Understanding the connection between words and symbols is a polished preacher's inheritance but also her or his stock-in-trade—so it must have seemed to Baldwin.

With this comprehension, this species of preacher will develop her or his voice—a necessity for engaging the complexities of evil outside the doors of the storefront and the cathedral. To be effective outside those doors, a polished preacher must be commissioned with a strong voice that proclaims Divinity's agenda. When a polished preacher pricks our consciousness, we see that the emergent kingdom of God is a transcendent presence and power (Matthew 13:44, ESV). The kingdom of God stands in direct opposition to the forces of an incumbent's power and empire.

Baldwin was among the first to see this trait in King. He must have known that King would emerge as a significant public figure. Of course, public figures are simultaneously popular and unpopular; in any case, King was a tour de force in contemporary culture. Strangely, Baldwin's and King's destinies were similar and dissimilar, like a metaphor.[16] Both were endowed with the power of words and symbols, yet they were dissimilar in that Baldwin seemed to know that a polished preacher will go to unlimited lengths to prevent further advancement of a stifling status quo. Baldwin also knew opponents will go to unlimited lengths to prevent a polished preacher from declaring divinely inspired truth claims. These lengths include physical annihilation.[17]

This is where Baldwin distanced himself from King. Baldwin was not called to preach living words. At first glance, his words and symbols seem similar to King's, but his convictions and demands for actions to be taken were dissimilar. Baldwin knew direct actions must be taken against imperial power and empire; however, Baldwin was not called to be a polished preacher, because fulfilling that calling may result in becoming a martyr. Baldwin was not a willing candidate for a martyr's crown. Baldwin and King as metaphor reveal human similarities and dissimilarities.[18] What is significant is that there are similarities and dissimilarities that demonstrate how metaphor functions. Later in this book we will take notice of this metaphoric process, which is the taproot of what is commonly known as metaphorical theology and is also key to grasping King's theology. For now, however, we remain focused on Baldwin's admiration of King and on King's living words.

The Endowments of a Polished Preacher

King as a polished preacher is a member of a rare species. Few are endowed with the mastery to command words and symbols that are divinely inspired to disrupt the status quo. As mentioned, this type of preacher has committed opponents who are both visible and invisible. King's visible opponents were mostly a part of the reactionary masses. His invisible opponents often were leaders who shaped public opinion or made public policies that affected people's livelihoods and were designed to create value gaps,[19] such as lack of access to health care and higher education, undemocratic control over people's bodies, and tyrannical incarceration of people's children.

To function in these arenas, all polished preachers must be endowed with unfounded courage to confront what can be rationalized only as unholy cosmic forces. For these reasons and surely others, Baldwin admired King. Living words demand action.[20] King's words and symbols were embodied in him and pointed toward the emergent kingdom of God. Words as symbols represent incarnation. Incarnational preaching points toward that which embodies the preacher, which is the transcending presence of Divinity, the person of Jesus of Nazareth. The Word has become flesh and dwelled among us (John 1:14).

Living Words and Symbols

King's words and symbols, I claim, are divinely inspired, and therefore he is commissioned to make apprehensible that Divinity continues to be enfleshed among us. In addition to salvation, Divinity's indwelling makes us aware of Advent. For example, Advent is a sign or symbol that something fleshly has happened. What has happened can be expressed only by words as symbols that function as representation and awareness of fleshly incarnation. Advent not only makes us aware of fleshly incarnation but also points toward the emergent kingdom of God. These events are one multidimensional event in the mind of Divinity.[21]

Baldwin realized, as I do, that King's words and symbols are filled with intrinsic and extrinsic worth.[22] A polished preacher of this caliber must be skillful to bend and manipulate words into symbols, just as ironworkers bend metals into usable objects. In King's case, by bending and manipulating words, he personified and set forth his beliefs and convictions. Thus, King fulfilled Baldwin's longing to witness a polished preacher. King's words were consequential; they empowered people to act. Thus, they were living words.[23]

King's living words gave voice to his theological claims, and his rhetoric reinforced his demands for action. Baldwin yearned to witness this. His polished King proclaimed courageously that Divinity demanded social and personal change (cf. Jeremiah 1:10). This Baldwin found morally and ethically attractive. King and Baldwin had theological claims, narrative, rhetoric, theology, and honesty in common. King, however, was assassinated because of these attributes while Baldwin was not.

Still, Baldwin's discernment was significant. He believed King embodied the transcendent presence and power of Divinity. What is more, King possessed courage to face foreseeable and unforeseeable challenges without a blueprint. As previously mentioned, a polished preacher may receive only sketches to fulfill her or his daunting assignments to build up or tear down (Jeremiah 1:8-10). In addition, Baldwin's polished preacher is a called preacher who is admired and respected because of being endowed with living words.

Living words are commonly known as metaphors. We will explore how metaphors or living words function in more depth in chapter 3. For now, I will place metaphor beside living words to reinforce my claim that King is a called, polished preacher, and offer an initial definition for metaphor:

> Metaphor is a startling juxtaposition of apparently unlike entities that initially provokes puzzlement, if not denial, in the reader or hearer. . . . Metaphor is primary language based on insights so peculiar that they cannot be cast into formulas and passed on. . . . Metaphor often combines an idea with the image of something material. . . . Metaphor is a mark of genius and therefore its use is not restricted to adults, the educated, or modern communicators.[24]

Careful readers recognize that the term *living words* is a metaphor for metaphor. A polished preacher uses metaphor to bend words into symbols that are combined with images of something that uncovers broader meaning.

Juxtaposition is a literary tool employed to help readers' awareness of images that include contrasts, comparisons, similarities, or dissimilarities: two things seen or placed together with contrasting effect. No person has been more skillful at using juxtaposition than the premier polished preacher, Jesus of Nazareth. Note, for example, his beatitudes: "Blessed are the poor in spirit, for theirs is the kingdom of heaven. Blessed are those who mourn, for they will be comforted. Blessed are the meek, for they will inherit the earth. Blessed are those who hunger and thirst for righteousness, for they will be filled. Blessed are the merciful, for they will receive mercy" (Matthew 5:3-7). Jesus' living words are an example of how metaphor functions and how it is used effectively. That is, Jesus' words fit the cultural context in order to attract his congregants to his gospel. Jesus' gospel announces that the emergent kingdom of God is visible to those who yearn to become citizens of Divinity's kingdom.

Jesus comforts the poor with the good news that they will become possessors of the kingdom of heaven, and he promises the mournful that they will be comforted. He declares that hungering and thirsting for righteousness is noble, and that those who offer mercy will receive mercy. This is an example of how preachers can use startling juxtaposition. It functions when a polished preacher places words together that create tension between dissimilar word pictures. Jesus of Nazareth is the premier model, and we can trace his model to Martin Luther King Jr. Like Jesus, King is a craftsperson of metaphors (living words).

Ethical Expectations

Shortly after their initial meeting, Baldwin heard King preach and observed, "He suffered with them [members of Dexter Avenue Baptist Church, Montgomery, Alabama] and thus, he helped them suffer. The joy which filled this church, therefore, was the joy achieved by people who have ceased to delude themselves about an intolerable situation, who have found their prayers for a leader miraculously answered, and who now know that they can change their situation, if they will."[25] Baldwin did not point to the Sermon on the Mount, but we can infer the similarities in Matthew 5:3-7.

Jesus clearly understands the human condition and, in this instance, that of the people in Nazareth and Capernaum. Jesus loved and served them, and they felt his solidarity with them. But Jesus did not pity his audience. Instead, he used poetic or living metaphors, which are living words. Like an ironworker, Jesus brilliantly manipulated and bent his words into living metaphors to present ethical expectations to the people. Ethical expectations here are like Baldwin's hope masquerading as dread.

Baldwin had become a witness to King's Jesus ethic.[26] He had attained further evidence that he had found his polished preacher. Baldwin witnessed King's suffering alongside his people and offered his version of hope in the future before his congregation without masquerading his hope as dread. King's living words are a demonstration of his mastery over words as symbols. What is more, we hear Baldwin's admiration of King, who embodied the transcending presence and power of Divinity and courage to face foreseeable and unforeseeable obstacles and adversaries. On these same lines, Baldwin shared his observations about King standing before his congregation:

> And surely, very few people had ever spoken to them as King spoke. King is a great speaker. The secret of his greatness does not lie in

> his voice or his presence or his manner, though it has something to do with all these. . . . The secret lies, I think, in his intimate knowledge of the people he is addressing, be they Black or white, and in the forthrightness with which he speaks of those things which hurt and baffle them. He does not offer any easy comfort, and this keeps his hearers absolutely tense. He allows them their self-respect—indeed, he insists on it.[27]

King was a great speaker, but I disagree with Baldwin about King's pulpit presence, which King possessed uniquely. I suggest that on this occasion King was sensitive to his congregation and therefore avoided speaking above their expectations. The pastor King knew his people and knew what they needed; he knew how to speak to those needs in a nonthreatening manner.

Prominent King scholars have been privileged to have access to the complete King canon, and it is clear that he had unusually rare capacities and mastery over words as symbols. This fact stands among the reasons that I have posited that Baldwin admired King. I assert that King functioned on this occasion as a parish pastor and spoke to his congregation in a pastor's tone. I believe he embodied a suffering servant and not a prophet or an orator on a public platform.

Earlier in this chapter I highlighted Baldwin's admission that his impromptu meeting caused him anxieties, but it also disturbed King's writing. As Baldwin mentioned, King lived in Montgomery, Alabama, and during that time King was writing *Stride toward Freedom*. The first excerpt below reinforces King's awareness that a pastor's tone signifies to the congregation what kind of listening is required for a specific sermon and occasion. The second passage is also focused on King's tone, but in it King was communicating in a distinctly different context. The passages underline that King understood his ministry contexts and that he disciplined himself to function within each separately to connect and communicate with care to enhance the people's understanding:

> That Saturday evening as I began going over my sermon, I was aware of a certain anxiety. Although I had preached many times before—having served as associate pastor of my father's church in Atlanta

> [Georgia] for four years, and having done all of the preaching there for three consecutive summers—I was very conscious this time that I was on trial. How could I best impress the congregation? Since the membership was educated and intelligent, should I attempt to interest it with a display of scholarship? Or should I preach just as I had always done, depending finally on the inspiration of the Spirit of God? I decided to follow the latter course. I said to myself, *Keep Martin Luther King in the background and God in the foreground and everything will be all right. Remember you are a channel of the gospel and not the source.*[28] King broadly understood and accepted his complex ministry context. On the one hand, King was a pastor-preacher. As a pastor, he carried out his pastoral duties which included performing baptisms, weddings, funerals, making convalescent visitations, and his pastoral preaching. On the other hand, King was prophet-preacher. As an example, King understood the significance of the United States Supreme Court ruling of 1957. The ruling then became federal law which overturned segregation of all government public spaces. The ruling was a deathblow to the Taney Court's "separate but equal" decision (*Plessy v. Ferguson 1896*).[29] With the abolishment of legally sanctioned segregation, King knew that in the future desegregation of such unjust laws would lead to equal rights like Black voters' rights.
>
> In these passages King personified his role as a polished preacher. We sense his humility. He understood that his oratory must fit the occasion and his congregation's expectations. Too often this is not the case; many preachers have mistaken egotism for inspiration.

King said that if people were impressed with his oratory, they may be more impressed with the orator than the gospel. This applies to preachers today. If people become impressed with their oratory, then the preachers' egotism usurps their inspiration and sole purpose for any church's gathering, which is to hear the gospel. This implies that many pastors do not speak to their congregation's needs (and endless needs are present in every congregation). Many people know the transcendent presence and power of Divinity when love is manifested. A polished preacher instinctively knows the congregation's expectation: that divine love will be embodied in a polished preacher.

In the second passage, King functioned as a prophet, and he employed words as symbols to communicate to his congregants in such a way that they could discern the significance of the occasion. Notice how King used juxtaposition, juxtaposing "separate-but-equal" with "freedom and equality." Separate but equal cannot be freedom and equality simultaneously. By this effective use of juxtaposition, we discover that only "equality" signifies love, whereas "freedom" signifies hegemonic legislation. Only "equality" signifies a democratic act. In a following chapter, we will explore closely how living words as metaphor function in King's canon and more narrowly how they function at an intersection between King's narrative, rhetoric, theology, and homiletic. For now, we turn to rhetoric and discuss King's skillful use of the art form, which is also science and a technique.

Rhetoric as Art, Science, and Technique

Aristotle claimed that rhetoric is a branch of ethics.[30] That is, rhetoric persuades people to make choices toward what is determined to be the highest good. Hugh Blair defines rhetoric as the power of eloquence,[31] and Kenneth Burke focuses on rhetoric's influence on human behavior, which organizes social structures.[32] Richard Lischer points toward rhetoric as a symbol of a speaker's character. In short, according to Lischer, rhetoric is used to persuade people to approve of the orator's credibility and thereby gain approval of her or his arguments.[33] Jacqueline Bacon explains that rhetoric has forms of signification (words that represent symbols).[34] Susan Jarratt suggests that rhetoric persuades narrative form.[35] Paul Ricoeur posits that rhetoric is a species of a trope (figurative speech) or living words we have identified and characterized as metaphors.[36] Importantly, rhetoric persuades that action be taken.[37]

All these definitions contribute to our understanding of how King's rhetoric functions, but Ricoeur's definition of rhetoric seems to be the closest to my understanding of King's rhetoric. I remind readers that King's rhetoric intersects with his narrative and his theology, which I later describe as his metaphorical theology (chapter 4). Rhetoric, like metaphor, informs the language of the oppressed, which is evident in Jesus' New Testament sayings, including his parables. This is discussed at length in chapter 5, but for now we focus on King's early exposure to the art form.

Martin Luther King Jr. was exposed to, impassioned by, and trained in classical rhetoric. One scholar writes that according to King family legend, the little boy King said to his mother, "When I grow up I'm going to get me some big words." And "like his father before him, Martin memorized passages from the King James Version of the Bible and practiced them until he had incorporated its Elizabethan cadence into his own pattern of speech."[38]

While King was young, he and other church friends were fascinated with the techniques of neighborhood preachers, similar to how jazz musicians are fascinated with older, experienced musicians. By studying preaching style and techniques, these young friends sought to discover and understand how preachers "wielded" power over their congregations. King's passion continued and evolved during his teenage years. Later King began his formal training in the art of rhetoric. Below is a brief example of the rhetoric used by the emergent King, a polished preacher:

> Nonviolence is a powerful and just weapon. It is a weapon unique in history, which cuts without wounding and ennobles the man or [woman] who wields it. It is a sword that heals. Both a practical and moral answer to the Negro's cry for justice, nonviolent direct action [the action to be taken is rhetoric] proved that it could win victories without losing wars, and so became the triumphant tactic of the Negro revolution [the emergent kingdom of God] in 1963.[39]

In chapter 3 we will explore other examples of how rhetoric is used by King.

Influences on King's Theology

Like that of most preachers and theologians, King's theology evolved and matured. As his theological depth expanded, he was able to create rhetorical space above his visible and invisible opponents. King's theology was birthed from his organic experiences and the language of the oppressed. King not only depended on the language of the oppressed but also used species of rhetoric to shape and form his theology to express, for example, the emergent kingdom of God.

Liberal Theology and Neoorthodoxy

Many if not most academicians and writers in the majority culture continue to focus on King's theology from their Eurocentric perspectives. This is understandable. King was trained at Boston University and Crozier Theological Seminary (now Colgate Rochester Crozier Divinity School). Colgate Rochester Crozier Divinity School boasts nearly two hundred years of Christian service in the evangelical liberal tradition and was a bastion of the social gospel movement. In later years, the institution self-described as an epicenter for Protestant progressivism.[40]

Such a luminary as Walter Rauschenbusch was a faculty member. In addition, Mordecai Wyatt Johnson, Howard Thurman, James A. Forbes Jr., Henry Beecher Hicks Jr., William Augustus Jones Jr., and Wyatt Tee Walker are graduates of the school. During King's time, his theological formation was the vocabulary of theological liberalism. King understood the differences between Eurocentric theological liberalism and his Black church grounding in the suffering of Black people:

> No matter how many times he repeated liberal platitudes about laws of human nature, morality, and history, King could not be a liberal because liberalism's Enlightenment vision of the harmony of humanity, nature, and God skips a step that is essential to the development of Black identity. It has little experience of the evil and suffering borne by enslaved and segregated people in America. Liberalism is ignorant—even innocent—of matters African American children understand before their seventeenth birthday.[41]

This is bifurcation, and it is not unique to King. Instead, King's bifurcation is consistent with that of many people of color, especially African Americans who attend Eurocentric institutions, theological or otherwise. When people of color and other marginalized statuses consider enrollment in the dominating culture's institutions, Eurocentrism is particularly concerning because those who teach in those institutions are conditioned by the biases of a Western worldview and the cultural traditions, customs, and biases of a specific institution. Whether knowingly or unknowingly, many professors project their biases onto students of all colors, genders, and other self-identities.

King was aware of such biases, but he made an intellectual and paradigm shift from his academic training in the traditions of white Protestant liberalism:

> The basic change in my thinking came when I began to question some of the theories that had been associated with so-called liberal theology. Of course there is one phase of liberalism that I hope to cherish always: its devotion to the search for truth, its insistence on an open and analytical mind, its refusal to abandon the best light of reason. Liberalism's contribution to the philological-historical criticism of biblical literature has been of immeasurable value and should be defended with religious and scientific passion. . . .
>
> The more I observed the tragedies of history and man's [human] shameful inclinations to choose the low road, the more I came to see the depths and strength of sin. My reading of the words of Reinhold Niebuhr made me aware of the complexity of human motives and the reality of sin on every level of man's [human] existence. Moreover, I came to recognize the complexity of man's [human] social involvement and the glaring reality of collective evil. I came to feel that liberalism had been all too sentimental concerning human nature and that it leaned toward a false idealism.[42]

King came to reject many major premises of neoorthodoxy as well. Whether theological formation is evangelical conservatism, Protestant liberalism, or neoorthodoxy, all are European constructs:

> So although liberalism left me unsatisfied on the question of the nature of man [human] , I found no refuge in neo-orthodoxy. I am now convinced that the truth about man [humanity] is found neither in liberalism nor in neo-orthodoxy. Each represents partial truth. . . . An adequate understanding of man [humanity] is found neither in the thesis of liberalism nor in the antithesis of neo-orthodoxy, but in a synthesis which reconciles the truths of both.[43]

For those who are trained and conditioned to invest in models of liberation theology, I suggest that we must exercise deliberate caution. Eurocentric beliefs and values are often informants for liberation theology, and therefore intellectual and spiritual suspicion is recommended.[44] Polished preachers who are called to serve within the Black church tradition may need to be reminded: we are to remain diligent about forming our own theologies for our contexts. The transcending presence and power of Divinity speaks and is recognized in our contexts, as William Augustus Jones Jr. rightly posits in *God in the Ghetto*.[45]

Philosophical Existentialism

King's paradigm shift continued beyond his formal training (he graduated long before Black liberation theology was birthed, but he was aware of its advent). Over time King's theological informant became philosophical existentialism. His reading included such luminaries as Martin Heidegger, Søren Kierkegaard, Friedrich Nietzsche, and Jean-Paul Sartre. These thinkers inform Black consciousness and complement Black liberation theology. We should continue to study these thinkers, but with informed caution.

However, social ethics as a discipline, with notable exceptions,[46] is overly represented by the majority culture's ethicists and theologians, many of whom study King's canon through their white gaze.[47] Nevertheless, it was King who may have made this attachment acceptable:

> Although most of my formal study during this decade [the 1950s] has been systematic theology and philosophy, I have become more and more interested in social ethics. Of course my concern for social problems was already substantial before the beginning of this decade. . . . I grew up abhorring segregation, considering it both rationally inexplicable and morally unjustifiable. . . . I grew up deeply conscious of varieties of injustice in our society.[48]

King's ethical worldview was approximate to theological ethics as much as social ethics. What is important is that King had to search for a school of thought and words that represented symbols for him to express further his divergent, evolving, and mature justice motifs. I point toward King's experiences during his childhood in Atlanta as an underlying informant. While a child, King yearned for justice, which later he would come to understand as social ethics and what we know to be theological ethics. Of theological ethics, I mean that we search for an ethical system that is beyond our current socio-human constructs and boundaries; social ethics then are often flawed and grounded in biases of Eurocentrism, which is the problem precisely.

King reasoned his way toward his expanding worldview, and knowingly or unknowingly, in order to ground his worldview, he accepted as an informant Georg Hegel's theoretical form: thesis-antithesis-synthesis.[49] I do not find this alarming. King neither claimed nor divorced himself completely from Western constructs. He could not have avoided Western biases and constructs (commonly known as Eurocentrism). However, I contend that polished preachers inside the Black church tradition should remain diligently aware and suspicious of Eurocentrism in all of its forms.

Again, liberation motifs were forming in the late 1960s. However, King rightly became suspicious about many theological premises, but, as I have demonstrated, he understood clearly that these were grounded in a limited, Eurocentric worldview. Thus, King became a forerunner in what is commonly known as practical theology, a Hegelian-like synthesis of conflicting and contradicting concepts that seek consensus. Hegel's model is studied in diverse fields, including theological studies.[50] Whatever the case, King's worldview continued to evolve and mature toward his emergent theology.

Toward a Metaphorical Theology

King was a master craftsperson of living words, words that represent symbols or metaphor. My position is that King's theology evolved and matured into a metaphorical theology. I think of theology as a conversation that Divinity is having with Divinity, and we are permitted and invited to eavesdrop on this transcending conversation. I add that Divinity speaks through the person of Jesus of Nazareth and the Spirit of Christ. This, I contend, is an accurate definition for revelation, which is a gift to individual believers and bodies of believers that we commonly think of as local church communities.

Still, I offer a more familiar and juried definition for theology. The following definition transforms our general description of eavesdropping on Divinity's conversations and places those conversations within a communal context:

> Black Theology must take seriously the reality of Black people—their life of suffering and humiliation. . . . When that man [or woman] is Black and lives in a society—permeated with white racist power, he [or she] can speak of God only from the perspective of the socio-economic and political conditions unique to Black people. Though the Christian doctrine of God must logically precede the doctrine of man [humanity], Black Theology knows that Black people can view God only through Black eyes that behold the brutalities of white racism. To ask them to assume a "higher" identity by denying their Blackness is to require them to accept a false identity and reject reality as they know it to be.[51]

This definition does not suggest that Divinity is beyond knowing. Instead, God-talk speaks directly to Black people about Black people's petitions and accepts our prayers, praise, devotion, and worship. In short, Divinity communes and fellowships with Black people, and we recognize the transcending presence and power of Divinity, as do others who make similar claims and develop similar beliefs. I further claim that others do not have exclusive, preferential God-talk treatments and statuses on such matters.

King's theology accepts, understands, and communicates to his congregations, his community, Blacks, and other socio-marginalized persons that Divinity understands their human suffering. What is more, King made attempts to share his theology of suffering with white oppressors who resisted admitting they were suffering from hatred, racism, and other immoral and unethical vices. Divinity, for King, is known through human suffering. In fact, if oppressors and oppressed people alike will not admit mutual suffering, reconciliation remains at variance.

Therefore, I do not agree with neo-orthodox theologians who theorize that Divinity is beyond knowing. Rather, I assert that Divinity is beyond words without symbols that represent the transcendent presence and power of Divinity. One religious scholar, Sallie McFague, makes a similar case:

> Increasingly, however, religious language is a problem for us, a problem of a somewhat different kind than the classical one. For most of us, it is not a question of being sure of God while being unsure of

> our language about God. Rather, we are unaware both at the experiential and expressive levels. We are unsure at the experiential level because we are, even the most religious of us, secular in ways our foremothers and forefathers were not. We do live in a sacramental universe in which the things of this world, its joys and catastrophes, harvests and famines, births and deaths, are understood as connected to and permeated by divine power and love. Our experience, our daily experience, is for the most part non-religious. Most of us go through days accepting our fortunes and explaining our world without direct reference to God. If we experience God at all it tends to be at a private level and in a sporadic way; the natural and public events of our world do not stand for or image God.[52]

Religious language continues to become a problem in our ever-increasingly secularized world. In more recent times, truth is unrecognizable to many people. In the United States, many conspiracy myths are on the rise. Polls suggest that many Americans did not believe that COVID-19 was a global pandemic, and thousands of people died due to the virus spreading across time zones, geographical locations, racial identities, and class stratifications. People of color were vastly and disproportionately affected by the virus; for many the infection proved deadly. This example lends itself to unbelief in democratic moral and ethical absolutes. It also signals a shift in conventional Western traditions and claims. This further indicates eroding claims of authority over defining sociopolitical and theological realities. It further indicates that religious language that depends on these eroding symbols is a casualty of the culture wars.

McFague focuses her attention on the image of God. That is, the image of Divinity has changed because words that once described the transcending presence and power of Divinity have increasingly followed secular ideas, and therefore our image of Divinity changes with those ideas. A polished preacher such as King must discover new ways to communicate biblical truth claims while a stabler set of rules replaces the outgoing ones. King's metaphorical theology was ahead of its time.

As a response and a corrective, we see King's theology as a rising model. King's model points toward the problem, which is religious language. King seemed to break from the stifling white gaze and status quo, and certainly by 1968, King, a polished preacher, affirmed our assertion when he spoke in the National Cathedral (Episcopal) in Washington, DC:

> I would like to use as a subject from which to preach this morning "Remaining awake through a great revolution." The text for the morning is found in the book of Revelation. There are two passages there that I would like to quote. . . . "Behold I [Divinity] make all things new, former things are passed away" . . . And I would like to deal with the challenges that we face today as a result of this triple revolution that is taking place in the world today. First, we are challenged to develop world perspective. No individual can live alone, no nation can live alone, and anyone who feels that he [or she] can live alone is sleeping through a revolution. . . . Modern man [and woman] through his [and her] scientific genius has been able to dwarf distance and place time in chains.... Secondly, we are challenged to eradicate the last vestiges of racial injustice from our nation. . . . I must say this morning that racial injustice is still the Black man's [and woman's] burden and the white man's [and woman's] shame. . . . [T]he vast majority of white Americans, spoken and unspoken, acknowledged and denied, ...the disease of racism permeates and poisons a whole body politic.... We are challenged to rid our nation and the world of poverty. Like a monstrous octopus, poverty spreads its nagging, prehensile tentacles into hamlets and villages all over the world.... They are ill-housed, they are ill-nourished, they are shabbily clad. I have seen it in Latin America; I've seen it in Africa; I've seen this poverty in Asia.[53]

King's first challenge was that a new global perspective points toward a new reality, which is that we are to become global citizens. This means we accept that all people are equal in the divine economy. These are living words, that is, a metaphor for the emergent kingdom of God.

However, some people, King indicated, have chosen to sleep through the revolution; more precisely, some people are asleep through the revelation of Divinity. Examples of the second challenge might be a lack of ethical, moral, and political will to transform unfair housing policies sanctioned by federal, state, and local governments, inaccessibility to universal health care, mass incarceration, and a need for immigration reforms and economic reparations.

A third challenge was King's passion to abolish global hunger, but abolishing hunger continues to elude world leaders and especially leaders of the United States.

Like Baldwin, we are attracted to King. King pursues truth on the same lines as Baldwin. Readers may grasp Baldwin's polished preacher's mastery over words that represent symbols. King's words and symbols together demand action that uncover the unwillingness of socioeconomic elites to end global hunger and poverty. Hunger and poverty predominately affect oppressed peoples, namely, people of color.

From the sermon excerpts, we notice that King's theology emerges as social ethics. His use of rhetorical juxtaposition is seamless and points us toward his theological underpinning: "scientific genius has been able to dwarf distance and place time in chains" can be interpreted as certain classes of people intentionally reinforcing economic slavery in the 1960s.[54] King implied that scientific advancements continued to occur much faster than culture could provide thoughtful, ethical critique of new advancements. By contrast and comparison, King demonstrated that scientific breakthroughs may be a boon to the global economy. At the same time, economic boons can be immoral, amoral, and unethical. For a polished preacher such as King, in fact, economic advances may be harmful to the welfare of global communities.

Another example of King's brilliant employment of juxtaposition is his language that underscores hypocrisy of false claims such as the so-called white man's burden. To make this clear to his listeners, he superbly disrupted conventional understandings by replacing the white man's burden with an unconventional claim. King knew that his audience would recognize immediately that he had read Rudyard Kipling's poem "White Man's Burden." King disrupted Kipling's poem and redirected his listeners toward his own ethical position. King wanted his audience to focus on the trappings of imperialism in order to have them face the white man's and woman's shame and guilt.

White guilt continues because some white people continue aggressively and passively to be conspirators of hegemonic policies that perpetuate systemic racism. For King, unbridled racism continued to permeate and poison the nation's body politic. A final example: King as a polished preacher pointed toward global poverty, which he witnessed in the global South—Asia and Africa. King inferred that this was a systemic matter; Eurocentrism was an unholy trinity of race, economics, and politics.[55]

James Baldwin's Search for Truth

I began with James Baldwin's search for truth, which I assert is the primary reason he sought to meet King. Baldwin was oriented to faith through the worst of the white gaze, namely, a Eurocentric Christian worldview that continues to perpetuate psychological slavery. Eurocentric Christian models reinforce deceitful white mythologies. In Baldwin's adolescent circles, Divinity was white. This was common then, and in Baldwin-like circles it is common today. Many Blacks in America, as well as many whites, still believe this lie.[56]

The lie includes Baldwin's view of Divinity, which was parochial. Divinity as liberator did not exist inside the doors of Baldwin's storefront church. His toxic Christian worldview did not provide even minimum space for hope, ambition, or confidence. A confident Black boy was dangerous to any dysfunctional ecosystem.

In fact, Baldwin's stepfather, Reverend David Baldwin, believed the lie and epitomized parochial fear of what lurked outside the doors of the storefront church:

> The fear that I heard in my [step]father's voice, for example, when he realized that I really *believed* I could do anything a white boy could do, and had every intention of proving it, was not at all like the fear I heard when one of us was ill or had fallen down stairs or strayed too far from the house. It was another fear, a fear that the child, in challenging the white world's assumptions, was putting himself in the path of destruction. . . . That summer, in any case, all the fears with which I had grown up, …like a wall between the world and me drove me, into the church.[57]

Elsewhere Baldwin conceded that his religious worldview was broadened over time. Baldwin admits his Christian worldview (and perhaps his sexuality) was not affirmed in his storefront church. His ambitious and audacious belief that he was equal to whites revealed his stepfather's fear. Baldwin's lack of fear of whites threatened his stepfather and exorcised his deeply felt anger about his human condition. It was his stepfather's fear that caused Baldwin to question whether either of them could be a polished preacher.

Baldwin's prophetic worldview threatened his fellow parishioners, as did his views that other socio-oppressed people's equality was possible. What is important here is that Baldwin questioned, interrogated, and over, time, resisted his culture and his inherited parochial religious worldview. Baldwin admitted, "I supposed Him [Divinity] only to exist within the walls of the church—in fact, of our church—and I supposed God and safety were synonymous. The word 'safety' brings us to the real meaning of the word 'religious' as we use it."[58] Baldwin's disappointment was religious language because, like so many others, he discovered its inadequacies to express Divinity's transcending presence and power in the emergent kingdom of God.

There was no doubt Baldwin was a promising and prodigious pulpiteer, but he became disillusioned. His faith crisis was multifaceted, and because his religious language was inadequate, like so many others, Baldwin did not mature religiously. His socioreligious culture was once again parochial:

> I was forced, reluctantly, to realize that the Bible had been written by men, and translated by men out of languages I could not read, and I was already, without quite admitting it to myself, terribly involved with the effort of putting words on paper. . . . And I also knew by now, alas, far more about divine inspiration than I dared admit, for I knew how I worked myself . . . into my own visions, and how frequently—indeed, incessantly—the visions God granted to me differed from the visions He [Divinity] granted to my father.[59]

Of course, the Bible (the Hebrew Bible and the Christian Bible) was written by men, but not white men (though some translators were white). Baldwin admits that his formation made him doubt the efficacy of his religious conversion. Baldwin's crisis was caused in large part because of his lack of exposure to and relations with literate preachers and teachers—women and men who were capable of nurturing Baldwin. The problem with religious language may have stunted Baldwin's theological worldview and possibly prevented him from becoming a polished preacher.

Baldwin recalls, "Shortly after I joined the church, I became a preacher—a Young Minister—and I remained in the pulpit for more than three years."[60] It is painful that Baldwin decided he would rather write than preach—and I concede this may have been destined for him. Still, Baldwin may have become a polished preacher. What follows is about his exit from his brief pulpit ministry:

> For his last sermon, Jimmy chose his stepfather's favorite text, "Set thy house in order." The right topic for nearly every reason, it was a farewell not only to the church but to his stepfather's house and to his old life. One day late in 1940, sitting on a park bench with Emile Capouya, Jimmy burst into tears and revealed that he was illegitimate. He learned this "terrible truth" about himself in a conversation between his parents. What he overheard he had vaguely suspected; it explained much of Mr. Baldwin's attitude toward him. His "father's" house was not his house. "Set thy house in order" was a call to the prophet within young James and the essence of the message he would soon carry as the "bastard of the West" into the house that was Western civilization at large, the house that had dispossessed him even as it had dispossessed his ancestors.[61]

After his sermon he left the building. In spite of the objections of the minister in charge, he joined Capouya on Forty-Second Street for a movie. The wider possibilities of the arts and the flesh won out over the narrowness of the church.[62]

It adds up. Baldwin knew what a polished preacher looked like. It was a person who possessed living words, words that represent symbols, words that demand action be taken. Words that led James Baldwin to Martin Luther King Jr.—the polished King.

Notes

1. James Baldwin, "The Dangerous Road before Martin Luther King," in *James Baldwin: Collected Essays*, ed. Toni Morrison (New York: Library of America, 1998), 638.

2. Lewis Baldwin, *There Is a Balm in Gilead: The Cultural Roots of Martin Luther King Jr.* (Minneapolis: Augsburg, 1992).

3. David Buttrick, *Preaching the New and Now* (Louisville, KY: Westminster John Knox, 1998), 15.

4. Sallie McFague, *Metaphoric Theology: Models of God in Religious Language* (Philadelphia: Fortress, 1982), 1.

5. John McClure, *Otherwise-Preaching: A Postmodern Ethic for Homiletics* (St. Louis, MO: Chalice, 2001), xi.

6. Eddie Glaude Jr., "The Lie," in *Begin Again: James Baldwin's America and Its Urgent Lessons for Our Own* (New York: Crown, 2020), 7.

7. Baldwin, "Dangerous Road," 638.

8. Baldwin, 638.

9. Kenneth Burke, *On Symbols and Society*, ed. Joseph R. Gusfield (Chicago: University of Chicago Press, 1985), 14. If we take Baldwin to be "the playwright, the poet, the sociologist . . . all human beings must make use of ways of framing or placing experience in order to make sense of it to themselves and to others." In short, Baldwin could see that the future for King was to be a drama that ended in tragedy.

10. David Leeming, *James Baldwin: A Biography* (New York: Arcade Publishing, 2015), 28.

11. James Baldwin, "Down at the Cross," in *James Baldwin: Collected Essays*, ed. Toni Morrison (New York: Library of America, 1998), 310.

12. Lane Cooper, ed., *The Rhetoric of Aristotle* (Englewood, NJ: Prentice-Hall, 1932), 8–9.

13. Karl Barth, *Church Dogmatics*, vol. 1 (New York: T&T Clark, 2010), 10.

14. Joseph Evans, *Lifting the Veil over Eurocentrism: The Du Boisian Hermeneutic of Double Consciousness* (Trenton, NJ: Africa World Press, 2014), 2.

15. Burke, *On Symbols and Society*, 158, 280.

16. George Lakoff and Mark Johnson, *Metaphors We Live By* (Chicago: University of Chicago Press, 1980), 1.

17. Martin Luther King Jr., "Why We Can't Wait," in *A Testament of Hope: The Essential Writings and Speeches of Martin Luther King Jr.*, ed. James M. Washington (New York: HarperOne, 1986), 542. Martin Luther King Jr. and Ralph Abernathy were jailed because they would go to any length to strive toward democratic justice: "We decided that Good Friday, because of its symbolic significance, would be the day that Ralph Abernathy and I would present our bodies as personal witnesses in this crusade."

18. Cooper, *Rhetoric of Aristotle*, 219. Metaphor intersects with rhetoric because it functions as a "vital activity."

19. Eddie Glaude Jr., *Democracy in Black: How Race Still Enslaves the American Soul* (New York: Broadway Books, 2016), 6.

20. Glaude.

21. Buttrick, *Preaching the New and Now*, 15.

22. Paul Ricoeur, *Interpretation Theory: Discourse and the Surplus Meaning* (Fort Worth: Texas Christian University Press, 1976), 48.

23. Similarly, see Jeremiah 1:6-10 to see how God provided Jeremiah with powerful living words.

24. Richard Lischer, *The Preacher King: Martin Luther King Jr. and the Word That Moved America* (Oxford: Oxford University Press, 1995), 118.

25. Baldwin, "Dangerous Road," 643–44.

26. Joseph Evans, *Reconciliation and Reparation: Preaching Economic Justice* (Valley Forge, PA: Judson, 2018), 77.

27. Baldwin, "Dangerous Road," 644.

28. Martin Luther King Jr., *Stride toward Freedom*, in *A Testament of Hope: The Essential Writings and Speeches of Martin Luther King Jr.*, ed. James M. Washington (New York: HarperOne, 1986), 419.

29. Martin Luther King Jr., "Give Us the Ballot," in *A Testament of Hope: The Essential Writings and Speeches of Martin Luther King Jr.*, ed. James M. Washington (New York: HarperOne, 1986), 197.

30. Cooper, *Rhetoric of Aristotle*, 9.

31. Hugh Blair, "Lecture XXV," in *Lectures on Rhetoric and Belles Lettres*, ed. Linda Ferreira-Buckley and S. Michael Halloran (Carbondale: Southern Illinois University Press, 2005), 264–65.

32. Burke, *On Symbols and Society*, 188.

33. Lischer, *Preacher King*, 120.

34. Jacqueline Bacon, *The Humblest May Stand Forth: Rhetoric, Empowerment, and Abolition* (Columbia: University of South Carolina Press, 2002), 9.

35. Susan Jarratt, "Ekphrastic Rhetoric and National Identity in Adam Smith's Rhetoric Lectures," in *Scottish Rhetoric and Its Influences*, ed. Lynn Lewis Gailett (Mahwah, NJ: Hermagoras, 1998), 46.

36. Ricoeur, *Interpretation Theory*, 47.

37. Burke, *On Symbols and Society*, 9, 23.

38. Lischer, *Preacher King*, 40.

39. Martin Luther King Jr., *Why We Can't Wait* (New York: Penguin, 2000), 16.

40. John R. Tyson, "The Strong Years," in *School of Prophets: A Bicentennial History of Colgate Rochester Crozer Divinity School* (Valley Forge, PA: Judson, 2019), 61–62.

41. Lischer, *Preacher King*, 53.

42. Martin Luther King Jr., "Pilgrimage to Nonviolence," in *A Testament of Hope: The Essential Writings and Speeches of Martin Luther King Jr.*, ed. James M. Washington (New York: HarperOne, 1986), 35–36.

43. King, "Pilgrimage to Nonviolence," 36.

44. James H. Cone, *Black Theology and Black Power* (Maryknoll, NY: Orbis, 2018), xxix.

45. William Augustus Jones Jr., *God in the Ghetto* (Elgin, IL: Progressive National Baptist Convention Press, 1979).

46. L. Baldwin, *Balm in Gilead*; and Emilie M. Townes, *Womanist Ethics and the Cultural Production of Evil* (New York: Palgrave, 2006).

47. Divinity has been made into the image, likeness, and identity of white males and, increasingly, white females. The image of Divinity has been interpreted through that white gaze, which is sanctioned by guardians of the status quo.

48. King, "Pilgrimage to Nonviolence," 36; L. Baldwin, *Balm in Gilead*; Townes, *Womanist Ethics*.

49. Georg Wilhelm Friedrich Hegel, *Phenomenology of Spirit* (Oxford: Oxford University Press, 1952), 2, 99.

50. Hegel.

51. Cone, *Black Theology and Black Power*, 132.

52. McFague, *Metaphoric Theology*, 1.
53. King, "Remaining Awake through a Great Revolution," 268–71.
54. King, "Remaining Awake through a Great Revolution," 269.
55. W. E. B. Du Bois, *Dusk of Dawn: An Essay toward an Autobiography of a Race Concept* (Piscataway, NJ: Transaction, 2011), ix.
56. Glaude, "The Lie," 7.
57. Baldwin, "Down at the Cross," 302.
58. Baldwin, "Down at the Cross," 305.
59. Baldwin, "Down at the Cross," 307.
60. Baldwin, "Down at the Cross," 296.
61. Leeming, *James Baldwin*, 31.
62. Leeming.

CHAPTER 2

King Confronted the Lie with His Metaphorical Process

> But the lie's most pernicious effect when it comes to our history is to malform events to fit the story whenever America's innocence is threatened by reality. When measured against our actions, the story we have told ourselves about America being a divinely sanctioned nation called to be a beacon of light and a moral force in the world is a lie. . . . The lie cuts deep into the American psyche. It secures our national innocence in the face of the ugliness and evil we have done.
> —Eddie S. Glaude Jr.[1]

Eddie Glaude tells a masterful story about the courageous witness of James Baldwin. The story of *Begin Again* reveals both Glaude's and Baldwin's creative and literary witness. Before we can begin, Glaude writes, America must face what he calls the lie. Glaude channels his inner Baldwin and contests Eurocentric archetypes and symbols that are representations of white supremacy. These claims have long been disguised as the romantic grandeur of a make-believe past.[2] An obvious example is the synthetic propaganda of the so-called Lost Cause—an alternative narrative invented and implemented to soften the treasonous failures of the Confederacy, its ideologies, values, beliefs, traditions, and culture.[3]

Although anachronistic, romantic grandeur as white mythology is an intentionally distorted revision of white America's unrelenting culture of violence and death. I ask readers to keep in mind, through this hermeneutic lens, that we interpret the lie as the culture of violence and death. White mythology then personifies the lie. In this way, we have been conditioned to romanticize our tawdry American past. It is our tawdry past that continues to haunt the American present. Anything that haunts is a nightmare, and for Americans, it has been our unrelenting nightmare.

Obstructions of Truth and Justice

Glaude's Baldwin saw through these nightmarish obstructions of truth and justice. And like Baldwin, Glaude holds his own mirror and courageously points it toward our public selves and offers reflection and critique to us about us. As a storyteller, Glaude is an informed master craftsman of critical race theory.[4] Like Baldwin, he knows that white mythology must be confronted. I point toward Baldwin's prophetic and edgy commentary on confronting and exposing the lie. Baldwin writes:

> The American Negro has the great advantage of having never believed that their ancestors were all freedom-loving heroes, that they were born in the greatest country the world has ever seen, or that Americans are invincible in battle and wise in peace, that Americans have always dealt honorably with Mexicans and Indians and all other neighbors or inferiors, that American men are the world's most direct and virile, that American women are pure. Negroes know far more about white Americans than that.[5]

Baldwin describes critical race theory, and the preceding quotation is an example of deconstruction of white mythology.[6] Baldwin then has made his contribution to both confronting and contesting white mythology, which I, alongside Glaude, characterize as the lie. Without question, the lie and white mythology are inseparable, and therefore it is our imperative to ensure that white mythology continues to be contested. If not, white mythology will continue to perpetuate.

White mythology is deliberately inaccurate and filled with misleading claims. We need only to revisit *The Birth of a Nation* (1915) and *Gone with the Wind* (1939).[7] As a component of propaganda, cinematography has a long history of reinforcing and disguising white mythology. It provides a dangerous representation and distortion of reality. Of course, white mythology is not reality. It is romantic tales—tales to be told but not to be believed.

Still, the lie has metastasized into our dysfunctional democratic culture and into our dysfunctional American psyche. I understand that we have attached dysfunctional democratic culture to our dysfunctional American psyche. But I am certain that white mythology is a cancerous pathology that threatens the life of the American experiment, which is our unending pursuit of a more perfect union. We seek a healthy democratic culture.

Democracy is charged to debate claims about truth and justice and to hear voices from the concerned and marginalized (and those who feel marginalized). The paradox, however, is that white mythology is quilted into the fabric of democratic culture, the public square, public opinion, public consciousness, and, as mentioned, the American psyche. These cannot be considered as separate viral strains. My description of our fragile democracy is similar to Jesus of Nazareth's parable (see Matthew 13:24-30), which I suggest is an example of accommodation culture: "Let both of them grow together until the harvest; and at harvest time I will tell the reapers, Collect the weeds first and bind them in bundles to be burned, but gather the wheat into my barn" (v. 30). A healthy democratic culture is also a species of accommodation. It seems that Jesus adroitly implied that to maintain democratic privileges, the democratic among us must accommodate the undemocratic. Reinforcing this thought is part of Jesus' High Priestly Prayer: "They [we] do not belong to the world, just as I do not belong to the world" (John 17:16). Jesus indicated that his disciples are not a part of the world order.

Said another way, democratic culture as accommodation culture and the American psyche are intertwined and manipulated to provide rhetorical spaces for propagandists who are committed to maintaining the lie. The Trump years bear witness to this claim. In horror the world witnessed brazen and desperate Trump supporters scale the citadel of the United States Capitol, our visible symbol of democracy. Their goal was to take back their country, even by treasonous actions against the republic for which it stands. (The irony could not go unnoticed: American chattel slaves built the Capitol building during the American Civil War.) These deceived rebels attempted to murder the then vice president, Mike Pence, and the speaker of the house, Nancy Pelosi. Their actions are representative of many others who believe the lie eases cultural pain.[8]

However, the lie does not arrest cultural pretentiousness and pride, nor does it unstiffen cultural shame, stains, and guilt. The lie does stiffen commitments to white mythology in order to retain undemocratic hegemonic advantages. White mythology thinly veils hegemonic advantages. Still, continuing an unrelenting pursuit of such advantages also continues to perpetuate deep generational and cultural behavioral dysfunctions. This is another justification for contesting and confronting undemocratic uprisings and underpinnings through democratic means. I caution that there are inherent risks involved in contesting and confronting the lie (white mythology and the culture of violence and death).

Those who confront white mythology also confront white privilege, fear, and rage. All are seamlessly woven into the fabric of the American psyche and pathos. By pathos, which shapes the American psyche, I mean dysfunctional ideas of romantic grandeur. We attach this to our dysfunctional American story. When the American story is threatened, fear and rage emerge. Carol Anderson's explanation for these irrationalities is profound: "The trigger for white rage, inevitably, is Black advancement. It is not the mere presence of Black people that is the problem; rather, it is Blackness with ambition, with drive, with purpose, with aspirations, and with demands for full and equal citizenship. It is Blackness that refuses to accept subjugation, to give up. A formidable array of policy assaults and legal contortions has consistently punished Black resilience, Black resolve."[9]

Black advancement stimulates white rage and continues a national addiction to white mythology. Black advancement also triggers white fear of Black revenge. Black advancement over and against obstructions of truth and justice such as the American slave institution, wealth and income disparities, Jim and Jane Crow laws, public lynching, inadequate housing, mass incarceration, and the like reveal cracks in white moral standing. As Glaude writes, "For both, the presence of Black people threatened the moral standing of the country and the moral character of its most valued assets—white Americans. White fear has never motivated people to look for solutions that would involve ameliorating the deep conditions that produced fear in the first place. Instead, the response has been to eliminate the fear by eliminating Black people."[10]

Glaude is correct to point out that white fear is an emotional response (i.e., guilt and shame) to socio-democratic, sociopolitical, and demographic changes. We cannot separate white mythology, the American psyche, and its pathos. In short, white America, which is addicted to white mythology, lives in delusional spaces and does not know it. Instead, the response of white America is unlike the courage of Baldwin or King. The presence of Black people threatens and exposes the lack of moral standing and character that is so pervasive in white America. Black presence disrupts white America's status quo. Black presence disturbs the romantic grandeur of the American dream. Not facing these challenges is disguised and veiled underneath the culture of violence and death. By definition, this is idolatrous worship of the lie (Deuteronomy 7:16).

To make sure the lie survives, the elimination of Blacks and other socio-marginalized people is preferred over truth and justice. Martin Luther King Jr. understood these tawdry conditions, many of which he experienced during his youth and others he faced during his brief adult life. Indeed, these conditions resulted in his death—an assassination that occurred on an infamous balcony in Memphis, Tennessee. Despite his looming and premature rendezvous with death, I agree with the assessment that King moved "the nation with the soul of the church . . . as a preacher moves a congregation."[11]

While King lived, he experienced and confronted that which I have characterized as obstructions of truth and justice. His experiences point toward his discovery of rhetoric and theology's agencies grounded in his metaphorical process. To metaphorical process, which up to this point has been defined as an intersection between rhetoric and theology, I now add living metaphor and how it functions in hermeneutics. Living metaphor provides intellectual space so that we are capable of understanding King's uses of living metaphor in various forms. Living metaphor can be interpreted as poetry, prose, and politics. Here I will expand on the definitions and employment of metaphor and how these have a significant presence and agency in King's hermeneutic, rhetoric, theology, and proclamation.[12]

Understanding the various forms of living metaphor helps us notice King's theological growth. As King continued to interpret his sociopolitical and socio-spiritual contexts, he began to evolve as a critical thinker. Readers know that critical thinking is important for developing an informed theological worldview. And as King's worldview evolved, his rhetoric, theology, and living metaphor informed his evolving metaphorical process.

King Confronted the Lie with His Metaphorical Process

Understanding that King's living metaphor is located between his rhetoric and his theology helps advance our understanding of his metaphorical process. Moreover, it helps us trace his maturation process. As King's metaphorical process evolves, it serves as a guidepost for us to follow his growth into his divine assignment. (In separate chapters of this book, I review King's rhetoric, theology, and homiletic, which are significant aspects of this metaphorical process.) His rhetoric gives shape to his theology, his theology informs his rhetoric, and living metaphor intersects both. Metaphorical process helps to explain how King communicated his public theology to both elites and masses in America and around the world.

In addition, we know that King's public theology was deliberately misrepresented and mischaracterized.[13] For example, Thomas Sugrue notes that Thomas Jackson, "a former researcher with the King Papers project at Stanford [University], has read King's every last sermon, speech, book, article and letter. What Jackson finds is that from the beginning of his ministry, King was far more radical, especially on matters of labor, poverty, and economic justice than we remember." The media "ignore[d] King's more radical pronouncements. They simply didn't fit into the developing story line."[14] (This included media of all philosophical and political leanings.) King, those around him, and many others understood deliberate, malicious attempts to distort his public theology and rhetoric, for his rhetoric was a demand for immediate action. Importantly, King understood the lie of white mythology.

In chapter 1 I underscored that James Baldwin, like the Greeks who sought to see Jesus during the Passover feast (John 12:20-26), sought to meet King. I believe that King was Baldwin's polished preacher. Already in this chapter, we saw Eddie Glaude give voice and clarity to Baldwin's prophetic contributions. Additionally, we noted that Anderson's definition of and explanation for white rage is its insistence to disrupt Black advancement. This is an indispensable insight into the dysfunctional American psyche.

Nevertheless, before the valuable scholarly works of Glaude and Anderson were published (and before either was born), Martin Luther King Jr. understood the emotional and psychological vice that continues to hold many religious and nonreligious white Americans (and Black, brown, and other socio-marginalized Americans) in its grip. King understood and experienced white fear and rage: "The first time that I was seated behind a curtain in a dining car I felt as if the curtain had been dropped on my selfhood. I had also learned that the inseparable twin of racial injustice is economic injustice. I saw how the systems of segregation ended up in the exploitation of the Negro as well as the poor whites. Through these early experiences I grew up deeply conscious of varieties in our society."[15]

Indeed, King described what W. E. B. Du Bois called double consciousness. Du Bois's definition clearly points toward pervasive psychological trauma, which here I associate with King as a representation of others. This psychological trauma and double consciousness are experienced by most if not all Blacks and other socio-marginalized people.

> It's a peculiar sensation, this double-consciousness, this sense of always looking at one's self through the eyes of others, of measuring one's soul [psyche] by the tape of a world that looks on in amused contempt and pity. One ever feels his twoness,—an American, a Negro; two souls, two thoughts, two unreconciled strivings; two warring ideals in one dark body, whose dogged strength alone keeps it from being torn asunder.[16]

Du Bois, King, and I have experienced the pervasive psychological grip of racism that surfaces through the dysfunctional culture of violence and death, which is a representation of the negative effects of the lie. The lie is white mythology's public face over what is cleverly hidden underneath. It covers white fear and rage.

Certainly, Martin Luther King Jr. understood that white fear and rage have tentacles that grip the collective life and anachronistic culture of oppressors. Their fear and rage are inflammatory, as it is becoming clearer by the day that incendiary rebels are losing their grip over an undemocratic culture. King knew that some would continue to perpetuate and peddle the lucrative but unethical and immoral trade of white mythology, which reinforces the lie. King also understood how the lie affects both the American psyche of the socio-marginalized and the dominating culture's democratic and undemocratic, religious, and nonreligious adherents. While the oppressed continue to make incremental liberation progress, the lie continues to cause psychic bruises.

King addresses white psychic bruises and insecurities that commonly manifest as obstruction of truth and justice. Often the result is violence and death:

> It would be grossly unfair to omit recognition of a minority of whites who genuinely want authentic equality. Their commitment is real, sincere, and is expressed in a thousand deeds. But they are balanced at the other end of the pole by the unregenerate segregationists who have declared that democracy is not worth having if it involves equality. The segregationist goal is the total reversal of all reforms, with reestablishment of naked oppression and if need be a native form of fascism.[17]

King's awareness of fascism influenced his use of language, or his metaphorical process.

Living Metaphor and the Black Preaching Tradition

A significant part of King's metaphorical process is living metaphor. Living metaphor holds meaning in tension. King's metaphorical process is effective because it causes tension; it confronts racist and fascist falsehoods and claims that are present in the American psyche. Living metaphor evokes contrasts and comparisons between one or more thoughts, worldviews, previously held perceptions, perspectives, and beliefs.

King was not the only Black preacher in the tradition who mastered employment of metaphorical process; most people reared in the Black church experience remain influenced by master preachers who use living metaphors. This is the metaphoric preacher:

> King was not acclaimed as a preacher for his mastery of generic sermon outlines. What moved his audiences were formulas and set pieces [his use of living metaphors and metaphorical process] he skillfully inserted into his sermons and speeches. The African-American preacher has at his or her disposal an enormous disassembled inventory of rhetorical parts ready for immediate installation. Some

> of the set pieces represent King's original composition; some he picked up by ear from the Black gospel tradition.[18]

King is among the inheritors of the Black church preaching tradition, and I underscore the organic use of living metaphors. However, King understood the role of metaphorical process on multiple levels. The role of living metaphor is linking ideas by way of symbols. In this instance, metaphorical process helped King make assertions that Divinity is personally present and recognizable in our human affairs and events (*Sitz im Leben*).

Later I will offer examples of King's use of living metaphor. Here I restate that white fear and rage served as chief informants for how King shaped his rhetoric, theology, and homiletics. Living metaphor functions as tension between two or more thoughts, ideas, or things. Living metaphors can cause tension between other living metaphors to disrupt conventional meaning and the status quo.

For example, King used the metaphorical process to become a spokesperson and defender for the oppressed against the oppressor's subjugating power. Living metaphor in King's metaphorical process hides the oppressed from the oppressor's white mythology, which is a representation of the lie. Remember that the romanticism of white mythology is violence, death, and the protection of a hegemonic culture. Not only does living metaphor replace and hide meaning, but it also can resurface as heroic symbols and images that represent oppressed people. In King's hands, metaphorical process made the oppressed visibly heroic and with the ability to face the oppressor. We see, then, the polished King understood the various forms and functions of living metaphor.

One significant feature of how living metaphor functions is what I call deferring understanding of meaning:

> Understanding of meaning may be deferred until an observer's comprehension is prepared to see and feel what is being placed before her or him as significant. I am aware that this is closely like reader-response and it may be. Reader-response often develops in communities of minds, those who share a similar worldview, preunderstanding, and social expectations. However, I know also that readers impose meaning into texts (and onto people) that is simply not there.[19]

Whether there are specific methods of interpretation that validate our understanding of meaning or deferred meaning, I am still not clear. Of import, there is minimal difference. I believe that King's use of living metaphor, which replaces and hides, functions psychologically with the consciousness of the oppressed and the oppressor. In this instance, living metaphor reveals dysfunctional belief in white mythology.

White mythology attached to the dysfunctional American pathology and psyche and double consciousness has historically prevented most auditors from hearing and accepting plain claims about truth and justice. Because of our collective dysfunction, it appears that the nation is at an impasse; put another way, America is near to losing its collective soul. Perhaps this parallels an episode located in Mark's gospel (8:32-37). The writer reports that people would not accept Jesus' willingness to tell them the plain truth. Peter, for example, preferred a lie over truth, and I suggest that Peter's dysfunctional behavior surfaced as I have aforementioned. Take notice of how it reads, "And He [Jesus] was stating the matter plainly. And Peter took Him aside to rebuke Him. But turning around and seeing His disciples, He rebuked Peter and said, "Get behind Me, Satan; for you are not setting your mind on God's purposes, but man's" (Mark 8:32-33 AMP).

I have grasped that Jesus was aware not only of the presence of Satan, but also of a dysfunctional pathology and psyche, and I add double consciousness which manifests as humanity's unwillingness to make collective and personal sacrifices. These forms of sacrifice are necessary in order to experience collective and personal salvation. This explains in brief verses 34-38. In short, Jesus gives his listeners a tutorial on salvific discipleship: "If anyone wishes to come after Me, he [and she] must deny himself [and herself] and take up his [and her] cross and follow me" (v. 34b). The passages continues with the following words located in verses 36-37. I have never read them without being emotionally disturbed, "For what does it benefit a man [and woman] to gain the whole world, and forfeit his [and her] soul? For what will a man [and a woman] give in exchange for his [or her] soul *and* eternal life?" These words describe collective and personal salvific sacrifice and the cost, which is self-denial and sacrifice for the whole of humanity.

I have attached Mark's gospel episode to our current cultural and social crisis. What is more, I suggests that it helps me to point toward the grave dangers of white mythology. At its taproot, white mythology, when uncovered, demonstrates that white America, like Peter according to Mark's gospel, is possessed with an unwillingness to accept truth and furthermore unwilling to make self-sacrifices. Instead, what manifests and emerges is a collective and personal dysfunctional double consciousness that functions to reinforce obstructions against truth and justice. The oppressor's double consciousness is similar to that which functions in those who are oppressed. Our example of this form of double consciousness is Mark's characterization of disciple Peter (Mark 8:32-37).

What is significant here is that Mark's episode helps us to understand the purposes King must have had in mind when he employed living metaphor. Throughout his public ministry, King used living metaphor to lift the curtain that had too long covered oppressive dysfunctional pathology and psyche and double consciousness. When these are present, human rage follows. White rage, I posit, is a result of unwavering belief and confidence in white mythology. However, as I have explained, underneath the rage exists dysfunctional pathology and psyche, and double consciousness. All manifest when many whites feel threatened as Anderson defines, "Black advancement." Even perceptions of Black advancement reveal white double consciousness triggered by white fear and rage.

Moreover, Black advancement threatens white mythology's intentional distortions. Indeed, Black advancement is an insurgence upon white mythology; furthermore, Black advancement has caused revisions that effect America's dysfunctional pathology and psyche. As James Baldwin made clear, Black folks "never believed" white mythology. Baldwin's assertion is plausible, but Black folks continue to have limited agency to disentangle themselves and others from the tentacles of white mythology. The Black church tradition has filled this agency gap.[20] This may be a reason why living metaphor finds a common place in the Black church's preaching tradition. It speaks to the oppressed about itself and about the oppressor simultaneously (both Black and white double consciousness function in the Black experience, often in a single worship service).

The employment of living metaphor by preachers in the Black church tradition is common. Nevertheless, the Black church experience has been taken for granted by some insiders who do not appreciate that which has been bequeathed to us. As a consequence, some insiders by birth do not understand, accept, or appreciate the cultural vanguard that is the Black church tradition. Not all who come from the womb of the Black church do not find her to be a shelter in a time of storm and a rock in a weary land.

Still, there are apprentices of our Black church tradition in the pew, choir stands, and other spaces who do understand and appreciate the experience and the privilege of their birthright. In King we see a legatee who understands his birthright and what has been bequeathed to him. King came to know this tradition as an apprentice, and during this period, he learned how to use living metaphor as artifice in his preaching. Later, as a seminarian, he formally came to understand the nature of metaphor and how living metaphor functions philosophically, aesthetically, and theologically. That is, at some point, King understood how living metaphor could be located syntactically at an intersection between his rhetoric, theology, and homiletic.

If we follow King's appropriation of living metaphor as a part of the metaphorical process, we, too, can appropriately use living metaphor. Skilled preachers and scholars using the metaphorical process position their heroines and heroes in the center of their narratives. This act establishes that polished preachers and scholars are the sole authorities over their narratives.[21] With living metaphor as the taproot of King's metaphorical process, he circumvented white mythology. Metaphorical process thus helps preachers to communicate their hermeneutic, rhetorical, theological, and homiletic claims to disrupt ethically the unethical conventional uses of language that are deliberate obstructions of truth and justice. We will return to this provocative assertion later in this chapter. For now, I advance my understanding of metaphorical process in general terms.

King's Metaphorical Process

In chapter 1 I introduced what I call living words. *Living words* is a metaphor for *living metaphor*, a significant part of metaphorical process. The metaphorical process that I will bring into focus later, I contend, is that of King. Seeing how living metaphors are interpreted in different contexts is important. I characterize these contexts as hermeneutic contexts (i.e., for rhetoric, theology, and homiletics, which I address in the next three chapters). Once we determine how to interpret contextually the function of living metaphor, we are able to trace and understand King's use of living metaphor. As I've said, King's living metaphors are located at an intersection between his hermeneutics, rhetoric, theology, and homiletics, which completes his metaphorical process.

Like a Venn diagram, rhetoric, theology, and homiletics overlap, and the imagery of the diagram makes the metaphorical process plain and easy to understand. Indeed, I have created a model that I allege is the polished King's model. Of course, his model depends on one's interpretation of the metaphorical process.

A metaphorical process shapes metaphorical thinking, and for King it meant prophetic thinking.[22] King's metaphorical process depends largely on how we interpret him. I define his metaphorical process to include a broad understanding of how living metaphor functions in different contexts. This can be precise as an appropriate use of living metaphor in individual sentences, paragraphs, and larger passages (for example, in some biblical passages).

Metaphor

Let us now provide background and definitions for metaphor. In chapter 1, I offered an initial definition that metaphor is startling and peculiar. In my view, metaphor points toward genius because it can be employed in various contexts and grasped by broad people groups.[23]

Still, metaphor is difficult to define because it is often described as dead: "The historical paradox of the problem of metaphor is that it reaches us via a discipline that died toward the middle of the nineteenth century," says one scholar.[24] Another scholar suggests that a metaphor functions in tension (dialectic), which often reveals irony: "Metaphor is a device for seeing something in terms of something else. It brings out the *thisness* of that, or the *thatness* of this."[25] I would add that metaphor is effective as much for what it does not say as for what it does.

A clearer definition of metaphor is provided by Sallie McFague, who has added to our understanding of how metaphor functions:

> Most simply, a metaphor is seeing one thing as something else, pretending "this is that" because we do not know how to think or talk

> about "this," so we use "that" as a way of saying something about it. Thinking metaphorically means spotting a thread of similarity between two dissimilar objects, events, or whatever, one of which is better known than the other, and using the better-known one as a way of speaking about the lesser-known.[26]

McFague makes a distinction between dead metaphor and living metaphor. A dead metaphor is identifiable in the use of ordinary language. That is, conventional language appears to have fixed meaning with little rhetorical space for broader interpretations. By contrast, living metaphor does not appear in ordinary language. Instead, living metaphor appears in extraordinary language and in unconventional ways. What is more, we cannot find living metaphor in a dictionary.

> Live metaphors are metaphors of invention within which the response to the discordance in the sentence is a new extension of meaning, although it is certainly true that such inventive metaphors tend to become dead metaphors through repetition. In such cases, the extended meaning becomes part of our lexicon and contributes to the polysemy (co-existence of multiple meanings) of the words in question whose everyday meanings are thereby augmented. There are no live metaphors in a dictionary.[27]

King frequently used living metaphor. One example appeared earlier in this chapter: "The first time that I was seated behind a curtain in a dining car I felt as if the curtain had been dropped on my selfhood. I . . . learned that the inseparable twin of racial injustice is economic injustice."[28] Straightaway, we grasp that living metaphor transforms familiar old images to make unfamiliar new images. The separating curtain of racial and economic injustice becomes visible by King's manipulation of the previous hegemonic meaning. What is also significant is that King's emotional trauma was hidden, but his use of living metaphor uncovered his trauma, making it visible. His emotional trauma was present while he was riding on a segregated train with segregated dining facilities. Separated by a curtain, which he reimagined and gave new meaning, he transformed the physical curtain, which represents white mythology, into a living metaphor. By using living metaphor, King makes clear, we see that white mythology is reinforced by the presence of the physical curtain. White mythology then represents unfair advantages which are unjustly sanctioned and reinforced by culture, traditions, and law. These are privileged advantages, privileges that retain and protect racial and socio-classist caste systems and suppress democratic rights and culture.

The oppressor, as I referenced earlier, has manipulated and exploited democracy to retain unfair advantages over fellow men and women of color. Keep in mind that segregation was legal and immoral separation. The physical curtain which I contend represents white mythology also represents emotional and psychological weight forced on the oppressed. King thus created his metaphor to point toward laws put in place to maintain others' dehumanization. Legal separation results in nothing less than collective trauma. This kind of trauma is antagonistic toward people of color and other socio-marginalized people. King's separating curtain is an excellent example of how we can use living metaphor to demand that action be taken toward human liberation.

King's living metaphor transforms our collective traumatized consciousness. His use of living metaphor provides necessary psychological (if not spiritual) space for immediate expression of the collective humiliation and pain of oppressed people. His living metaphor is effective because he used it to highlight old and new images, similarities, and dissimilarities. Living metaphor, by function and nature, creates new or different interpretations that we associate with poetry and new and or different evidence we associate with prose. Each points toward reality. Because King's living metaphor is located in an intersection, we witness how the oppressed invisible personhood that is hidden from the oppressor emerges and becomes a visible presence.

King commandeered the separating curtain and took its original meaning from the oppressor. He took authority over the separating curtain and created new and different meaning. King did not accept white supremacy and mythology as the last word. Instead, he resisted white mythology's intention, which is to maintain and finish Black folks' dehumanization. We cannot overlook that Black folks are at risk of global genocide. There is no denial that universally, Black folks have minimal access to adequate healthcare and experience human disparities, such as shortages of drinking water, and survive and live in solvable food deserts. These are our contemporary separating curtains. I suggest that readers grasp King's living metaphor and how it overpowers and redefines evil as racial and economic injustice, which are inseparable, even in our time.

King's critical memory about his traumatic experience is Du Boisian. Du Bois recounted his experience in Germany while he attended Wilhelm University (University of Berlin). While in Germany, he began to develop his construct of race, economics, and politics, which is a parallel parent of current critical race theory. Although this occurs in a different era than King's, it is similar. Du Bois wrote, "I began to see the race problem in America, the problem of the peoples of Africa and Asia and the political development of Europe as one. I began to unite my economics and politics; but I still assumed that in these groups of activities and forces, the political realm was dominant."[29]

Du Bois understood that race, economics, and politics are inseparable and used intentionally to create a web of oppression. The invisible web is spun to entangle Black folks and others. It is representative of a hegemonic construct that distorts what the polished King called selfhood (more commonly known as personhood). Now that we have seen an example of how living metaphor functions, let us consider ways to interpret it. This means we must recognize living metaphor and its functions in hermeneutical contexts. We narrow our scope here to these three forms of living metaphor and how each functions—poetry, prose, and politics.

Poetry

Poetry is a genre. If we understand this, we can interpret poems in their hermeneutical context. It is style, then, that helps the polished preacher and others to interpret a writer's or orator's intent. If we can interpret the poet's style, we can interpret his or her poetry.

> In poetics it is settled that good style is, first of all, clear. . . . The proof is that language which does not convey a clear meaning fails to perform the very function of language. . . . These deviations from ordinary usage make the style more impressive. Words are like men; as we feel a difference between people from afar and our fellow townsmen, so is it with our feeling for language. And hence it is

> well to give the ordinary idiom an air of remoteness, the hearers are struck by what is out of the way, and like what strikes them.[30]

Straightaway we follow the rules. First, we interpret the poet's style. Second, we interpret how the poet's style effectively moves hearers or readers to act. Third, we interpret the intersection between poetry and rhetoric. Poetry intersects with our claim. Like rhetoric, poetry demands that action be taken.

For action to be taken, brilliant poets give voice to the character of the action through their words, which are transformed into living metaphor. A poem's living metaphor opens human imagination to consider possibilities beyond the conventional interpretations of oral, social, and experiencing texts. Poetry then expands our recognition that Divinity is present in all realms of spiritual and human reality. This is important for Black folks and other socio-marginalized communities. We must sense a broader understanding of self and how we are perceived and how we perceive our worlds. Second, and intersecting with the first, we notice that poetry is effective when it deviates from ordinary language and becomes extraordinary language. This creates space for poets and polished preachers to expand our expectations. In short, we anticipate new dimensions of meaning.

A brilliant poet, Amanda Gorman is the youngest inaugural poet laureate in American history. During the Biden presidential inaugural ceremony, Gorman delivered her prophetic poem "The Hill We Climb." The poem defines the meaning of democratic leanings and expresses hopes, dreams, and yearnings for a democratic future. It also defines what is not democracy. Gorman's poem serves as an example of how living metaphor functions as poetics or simply as poetry. We turn to this definition of poetry to further grasp its function: "Poetry does not seek to prove anything at all: it as a project is mimetic [imitation]; its aim . . . is to compose an essential representation of human actions; its appropriate method is to speak the truth by means of fiction, fable, and tragic *muthos* [reality]."[31] This definition is true in general if not in frequent cases. However, as mentioned, I see Gorman's work as an example of how living metaphor represents human action to be taken.

Gorman's poem begins with a probing existential question: "When day comes, we ask ourselves where can we find light in this never-ending shade?" She does not ask her readers to answer her question without providing a supportive guidepost. By using her opening question as a guidepost, Gorman supposes that her readers will permit her rhetorical space to answer the question at some point during the poem. She does: "We've braved the belly of the beast. We've learned that quiet isn't always peace." Gorman's strategy then is to help readers grasp her intended meaning of the first three lines of her poem. We take notice that the three opening lines are to be read and interpreted together. This indicates the need to understand how hermeneutics function in a metaphorical process. We must interpret the writer's or orator's intent for her or his words. In this case, we are trying to interpret how living metaphor functions hermeneutically as in poetry in a metaphorical process.

Gorman's opening lines create an alliteration that echoes an episode in the Hebrew tradition. I attach her alliteration to the story of Jonah in the belly of the fish. Whether Gorman has thought of this specific biblical character, it is clear that stylistically she does allude to biblical imagery. To compare and contrast, I have included the first four lines of "The Hill We Climb" and Jonah 2:1-6 to support my claim.

Gorman:

When day comes: we ask ourselves where can we find light in this never-ending shade?
The loss we carry, a sea we must wade.
We've braved the belly of the beast.
We've learned that quiet isn't always peace.[32]

The writer of Jonah:

Then Jonah prayed to the Lord his God from the belly of the fish, saying,
"I called out to the Lord, out of my distress,
    and he answered me;
out of the belly of Sheol [the grave] I cried,
and you heard my voice.
You cast me into the deep,
    into the heart of the seas,
    and the flood surrounded me;

all your waves and your billows
  passed over me.
Then I said, 'I am driven away
from your sight;
how shall I look again
  upon your holy temple?'
The waters closed in over me;
  the deep surrounded me;
weeds were wrapped around my head
  at the roots of the mountains.
I went down to the land
  whose bars closed upon me forever;
yet you brought up my life from the Pit,
O LORD my God."
—Jonah 2:1-6

Gorman's words intersect with the words of Jonah. If we can accept that her allusion to the belly of the beast is similar to the belly of the fish, we have a glimpse into her rhetorical strategy. We know that the biblical Jonah did not want to prophesy and proclaim a warning message to the city of Nineveh. Instead, Jonah wanted to flee the presence of Divinity (Jonah 1:1-3).

Though the Ninevites were not necessarily an immediate threat to the Hebrew nation during the time of the writing of the book of Jonah (732 BC), the Ninevites were citizens of the Assyrian Empire. Historically, this nation-state was an oppressor and antagonist of the Hebrew people. To further dramatize Jonah's mistrust of the Ninevites, I compare what I imagine to be his psychological state of mind as something similar to this farcical notion: Divinity has told Albert Einstein to agree that his daughter will marry a son of Adolf Hitler. This I believe accurately characterizes Jonah's trauma and unwillingness to proclaim warning to those he believed to be an unsavory and unredeemable people.

Jonah's dread was sharing Divinity's words with the Ninevites precisely because he did not want to build relations between Israel and the Ninevites. In short, Jonah serves as a portrait of the Hebrew people's dread and suffering that are endured to survive, a dread caused by their historical oppressors.

What is more, we see a portrait of a forgiving and redeeming Divinity—even to our historic oppressors.

In like manner, Gorman's opening three lines can be interpreted as a portrait of Black dread and suffering. We endure pain in order to survive. The character Jonah, representing ancient Israel, is called to preach repentance to his nation's historical oppressors. I suggest that Gorman's intention was to create a living portrait that is set in a land that is never without shadows.

Where there are shadows, there is nearly absence of light. This means that Gorman's poem begins with our struggle to survive nihilistic darkness, a sense of nothingness, a near absence of light: "The waters closed in over me to take my life; the deep surrounded me; weeds were wrapped about my head at the roots of the mountains" (Jonah 2:5-6, ESV). And this is similar to a skewed psychological state of mind among Black people:

> The liberal/conservative discussion conceals the most basic issue now facing Black America: the nihilistic threat to its very existence. This threat is not simply a matter of relative economic deprivation and political powerlessness . . . it is primarily a question of speaking to the profound sense of psychological depression, personal worthlessness, and social despair so widespread in Black America.[33]

With this comment, Cornel West proclaims eerily that Black folks and other socio-marginalized people are to remain suspicious of dominating cultures' and classes' truth claims. In short, our answers have not and will not come from the American-Eurocentric religious-political conventional worldview, which is Eurocentric liberal and conservative ideologies. In addition, America's hegemonic construct does not permit democratic debate from otherwise people. By this I mean, socio-marginalized people of color who are made to feel invisible and therefore overlooked by many Eurocentric writers. Traditionally, these writers are focused on ideas that solely support their hegemonic Eurocentric ideals, cultural traditions, and mores.[34] When we consider our current economic deprivation and political powerlessness, this is obvious. More to the point, we continue to experience collective dread and suffering in the first quarter of the twenty-first century. For many Blacks and other socio-marginalized folks, we live inside the weedy, dark belly of the beast.

Prose

Prose is another genre, and we can interpret prose by investigating its style. In poetry, prose is spoken in rhythm.

> The pattern [*schema*] of diction should be neither metrical nor devoid of rhythm. A metrical [cadenced] structure makes the hearer distrustful by manifest artifice, and at the same time distracts his [or her] attention, making him [or her] watch for the reoccurrence of the beat. . . . Accordingly, prose should be rhythmical, or we shall have, not prose, but verse. Its rhythm, however, must not be too precise—must be carried so far and no farther.[35]

Aristotle had heard neither a Black preacher nor a Black poet, and neither had Aristotle witnessed their use of prose in a rhythmic cadence. Prose is a pedestrian language and rather ordinary, perhaps because it is meant to be clearly understood. However, when pedestrian language is spoken with a rhythmic cadence, it highlights poetry's extraordinary language. Still, prose is earthier than poetry, but a poem may include forms of prose.

Often prose grounds particular truth claims, but not by imitation of reality: as was stated earlier, poetry's "project is mimetic [imitation]; its aim . . . is to speak the truth by means of fiction, fable, and tragic *muthos* [reality]."[36] Once again, we return to Gorman's "The Hill We Climb" and look at her use of prose.

> We are striving to forge our union with purpose.
>
> To compose a country committed to all cultures, colors, characters, and conditions of man.
>
> And so we lift our gazes not to what stands between us, but what stands before us.
>
> We close the divide because we know, to put our future first, we must first put our differences aside.

I believe that Gorman has avoided dead metaphor. Although I characterize these lines from her poem as prose, her prose is forward leaning.

That is, her language is meant to acknowledge that we continue to face hegemonic divisions. But I further suggest her prose is instructive; we must move forward to the future. "Future first," then, is an ethical imperative.

Gorman's words are meant to be persuasive, and therefore we see an intersection with rhetoric's demand that action be taken. It is as though she is saying we must choose the highest good; we must accept each other, and we must work together. This is an ethical imperative. In this instance, her words are living metaphor, but her words remain pedestrian, plain, and clear. We are made to wait for Gorman's next rhetorical flight. However, her words are spoken with careful diction and with a deliberate rhythmic pattern, and her pedestrian words are highly effective. "We are striving. . . . committed to all cultures, colors, characters . . . conditions. . . . we lift our gazes not to what stands between us, but . . . before us. We close . . . we know . . . future first. . . ." This is a brilliant example of how prose can function in poetry.

For comparison, I include an excerpt from Martin Luther King Jr. that demonstrates how he uses living metaphor in his sentence structures that highlight his prose: "There [is] evidence that the [social] Revolution is now ripping into roots. For too long the depth of racism in American life has been underestimated. The surgery to extract it is necessarily complex and detailed. As a beginning it is important to x-ray our history and reveal the full extent of the disease."[37]

These lines are located in "The Summer of Our Discontent." King created living metaphor that perhaps was inspired by Shakespeare's phrase "the winter of our discontent" in *Richard III*. In both instances, the coldness of winter and the balmy heat of summer cause anxieties and restlessness. King's prose is brilliantly employed: "Evidence [of] the Revolution is . . . ripping into roots. . . . Racism has been underestimated. The surgery to extract it is . . . complex and detailed. . . . it is important to x-ray our history and reveal the full extent of the disease."

King's words are symmetrical, balanced, pedestrian, plain, and clearly understood. Furthermore, his prose is a species of style, and therefore we interpret his words as factual evidence rooted in reality. "Ripping into roots" could be a living metaphor that compares racism with a decaying, abscessed tooth and the severity of its bodily damage that has been underestimated. To paraphrase: We need an x-ray, King continued, of our American history to reveal the full extent of the disease, which is racism. King's words are metrical and have rhythmic cadence. This is prose, plainly syntactical and pedestrian.

Politics

Finally, politics is yet another genre. Living metaphor as political metaphor is an interpretation of that style, and the hermeneutical context is a species of political living metaphor. Like rhetoric, politics is the art of persuasion. This is a simple definition, but it helps readers see the intersection between living metaphor, politics, and rhetoric. The following excerpt supports our understanding of the nature of the political living metaphor: "Rhetoric is a kind of offshoot, on the one hand, of Dialectic [contentious speech, debate, and argument], and on the other, of that study of Ethics which may properly be called political. And hence it is that Rhetoric, and those who profess it, slip into the guise of Politics."[38]

Politics, according to Aristotle, is akin to the discipline of ethics. Ethics, for Aristotle, is the science dealing with individual conduct. I understand it to mean agreed-upon rules and expectations that define conduct. Or as Aristotle points out, individual conduct is ethics because it underscores the personal and public character of the orator and the writer. (For Aristotle, ethics shades off into politics, a broader subject that deals with the conduct and activities of people in groups—the state.)

In this context our concern is how we learn to look for the ethical nature of the oral and written composition of the polished preacher, poet, and politician. That is, we make an attempt to understand how orators and writers transform political living metaphor into political and ethical statements. I have located political living metaphor in another excerpt from Gorman's inaugural poem:

> Somehow we've weathered and witnessed a nation that isn't broken, but simply unfinished.
>
> We, the successors of a country and a time where a skinny Black girl descended from slaves and raised by a single mother can dream of becoming president.

Gorman's political living metaphor is prophetic because it appears to have foreshadowed the treasonous insurrection that occurred on January 6, 2021. Her metaphor represents an open window of insight into the daily thoughts, anxieties, and fears of socio-marginalized people across the world. Indeed, Gorman sees the dysfunctional aspects of our national psyche. The nation's dysfunctional psyche underscores a threat to the survival of an already fragile democracy. Still, Gorman reminds Black folks and some others that despite the continuous dogged struggle to retain self-respect, dignity, and sanity, the world hears that Black folks have endured the nation's dysfunctional psyche: "Somehow we've weathered and witnessed a nation that isn't broken." Here metaphor then symbolizes that the American public and global citizens witnessed an insurrection planned, organized, and executed by a mob led by confederated American citizens against the institutions of the United States. Gorman's political metaphor is powerful; it represents an inclusive democratic life, however fragile it appears to be in its embryonic form. Like King's emergent Kingdom of God in the earth realm, another way to express an inclusive democratic culture, Gorman's metaphor helps all of us to see it. A new democratic culture according to Gorman is coming, and through her eyes, we see it—this emergent democracy.

Here Gorman's political living metaphor—"a nation that isn't broken, but simply unfinished"—is similar to that of King's "separating curtain." This clearly is a species of political living metaphor that signifies failed resistance and raging unacceptance of the legal outcome of the 2020 presidential election predominately by white Americans. Gorman highlights that white mythology manifests as white privilege, double consciousness, white fear, and rage. The latter were on full display on January 6, 2021. These are manifestations of unhealthy hegemonic constructs. Gorman argues that we have weathered and witnessed; however, the nation is not broken, "but simply unfinished." Gorman offers another political living metaphor that points toward dogged progress. This living metaphor is forward leaning: "We, the successors of a country and a time where a skinny Black girl descended from slaves and raised by a single mother can dream of becoming president." Gorman has brilliantly spoken of democratic leanings, and she envisions a democratic future.

Gorman's prose is meant to be read as a poetic cadence that I suggest parallels Martin Luther King's cadence and his critical insight which I have located in his introduction to "The Summer of Our Discontent." I have included a lengthy excerpt so as not to interrupt the pedestrian, rhythmic cadence of King's style, which I have determined is his use of political living metaphor.

> More than twenty-five years ago, one of the southern states adopted a new method of capital punishment. Poison gas supplanted the gallows. In its earliest stages, a microphone was placed inside the sealed death chamber so that scientific observers might hear the words of a dying prisoner to judge how the human reacted in this novel situation. . . . The first victim was a young Negro. As the pellet dropped into the container, and the gas curled upward, through the microphone came these words: "Save me, Joe Louis. Save me, Joe Louis, Joe Louis. . . ." It is heartbreaking enough to ponder the last words of any person dying by force. It is even more poignant to contemplate the words of this boy, because they reveal the helplessness, the loneliness and profound despair of Negroes in that period. The condemned young Negro, groping for someone who might care for him, and had power enough to rescue him, found only the heavyweight boxing champion of the world. Joe Louis could do something because he was a fighter. In a few words the dying man had written a social commentary. Not God, not government, not charitably minded white men, but a Negro who was the world's most expert fighter, in this last extremity, was the last hope.[39]

This excerpt is filled with a species of political living metaphor. King brilliantly painted a political portrait with vivid characters that reinforce the culture of violence and death. Through King's prose, we see the culture's tawdry manifestations of white privilege. Looking into the death chamber are scientists, King wrote, observing a person's death like he is a laboratory rat and not a man. We hear a dying man calling for his Black hero—Joe Louis. King's story underscores that the young man is representative of Blacks and socio-marginalized folks who do not have confidence in a hegemonic government or a hegemonic Divinity. Instead, the Negro victim's hope was in "the world's most expert fighter." King's protest against capital punishment and the living metaphor signify political inequities and inequalities that are associated with capital punishment: "Poison gas supplanted the gallows." Throughout the next chapters, we will pay close attention to King's employment of living metaphors as poetry, prose, and politics that are present in his rhetoric, theology, and homiletic.

Mastering living metaphor is an ongoing process for most of us. I am certain that King mastered the art and science of living metaphor, and perhaps for a single and primary reason: King sought to deconstruct the lie which is white mythology. He understood the grip and grasp white mythology had and continues to have over the American psyche. When the majorities of whites and Blacks are emotionally and psychologically entangled in this hegemonic web, communicating truth claims is nearly impossible. There are many examples to this effect within the King canon. King was a master of oral and written communication and understood that the metaphorical process involves the cognitive and spiritual power of living metaphors.

Throughout this book we will witness his living metaphor and how it intersects between King's rhetoric, theology, and homiletic. In addition, we need to remember that we must interpret how living metaphor functions in context. I have suggested that living metaphor has distinct styles: poetry, prose, and politics. I am sure there are many others, but what I have provided is a guidepost. Last, interpretation is an art and science that is formally called hermeneutics. Thus, I have attached to King a metaphorical process that functions as hermeneutics, rhetoric, theology, and homiletic. For now, let us turn to rhetoric.

Notes

1. Eddie S. Glaude Jr., *Begin Again: James Baldwin's America and Its Urgent Lessons for Our Own* (New York: Crown, 2020), 8–9.

2. David E. Johnson, *Douglass Southall Freeman* (Gretna, LA: Pelican, 2002). Johnson writes boldly and courageously about Douglass Southall Freeman, a scholar at the University of Richmond, who is perhaps the architect behind the idea of the Lost Cause.

3. See Douglass Southall Freeman, *R. E. Lee* (New York: Simon and Schuster, 1991). By 1934, when the first edition of this book was published, Freeman had perfected the romantic idea that supports the losing Confederacy and reframes the treasonous character of Robert E. Lee.

4. See Richard Delgado and Jean Stefancic, *Critical Race Theory: An Introduction* (New York: New York University Press, 2017).

5. Eddie Glaude Jr., *Democracy in Black: How Race Still Enslaves the American Soul* (New York: Broadway, 2017), 39.

6. See Simon Critchley, *The Ethics of Deconstruction: Derrida and Levinas* (Edinburgh:

University of Edinburgh Press, 2014), 3; Henry Louis Gates Jr., ed., *Black Literature: Black Literary Theory* (New York: Routledge, 2017), 105–26.

7. Cass R. Sunstein, "Finding Humanity in *Gone with the Wind*," *The Atlantic*, July 16, 2015: "At this point, skeptics might respond that subsuming the actual politics of the war, and the pro-slavery convictions of the Confederacy, beneath the gauzy romance of the plantation is precisely what the Lost Cause has been about—that in the end, *Gone with the Wind* is inescapably a set of political claims, designed to promote political ends." See http// www.theatlantic.com//politcs/archives/2015/07/gone-with-thewind//confederacy/398663/, accessed on 9/12/2021. (Of course, the objective of political ends is to support deliberate agendas. In the case of antebellum America and our current circumstances in America, political ends have maintained racial and class advantages.)

8. See Peter Jones, "Pence and Other Officials Were Marked for Assassination," *International Business Times*, January 15, 2021, https://www.ibtimes.com/pence-other-officials-were-marked-assassination-3123425 and Salvador Hernandez, "A Man Who Threatened to Shoot Nancy Pelosi in the Head on Live TV Has Pleaded Guilty," *Buzzfeed News*, September 10, 2021, https://www.yahoo.com/entertainment/man-threatened-shoot-nancy-pelosi-200733426.

9. Carol Anderson, *White Rage: The Unspoken Truth of Our Racial Divide* (New York: Bloomsbury, 2016), 3.

10. Glaude, *Democracy in Black*, 39.

11. Richard Lischer, *The Preacher King: Martin Luther King Jr. and the Word That Moved America* (Oxford: Oxford University Press, 1995), 3.

12. Cleophus J. Larue, *The Heart of Black Preaching* (Louisville, KY: Westminster John Knox, 2000), 27–29. Larue provides a thorough analysis on the rules and functions of metaphors. What we call living metaphors, Larue describes more conventionally as extended metaphors.

13. Houston A. Baker, "Critical Memory and the Black Public Sphere," in *The Black Public Sphere: A Public Culture Book* (Chicago: University of Chicago Press, 1995), 16. Baker writes, "In so many ways, the language, the voice, the articulation of Martin Luther King, Jr. captures the peculiar agency of civil rights and the movement's effort to recapture and recode all existing American arrangements of publicness. King's voice and language made fully visible and audible the Black public sphere in America. He is, in fact, the King of the public counterpublic."

14. Thomas J. Sugrue, "Restoring King," *Jacobin*, January 18, 2016, https://www.jacobin mag.com /2016/01/restoring-king/.

15. Martin Luther King Jr., "Pilgrimage to Nonviolence," in *A Testament of Hope: The Essential Writings and Speeches of Martin Luther King Jr.*, ed. James M. Washington (New York: HarperOne, 1986), 37.

16. W. E. B. Du Bois, "Of Our Spiritual Striving," in *The Souls of Black Folk* (New York: Bantam, 1989), 3.

17. Martin Luther King Jr., *Where Do We Go from Here: Chaos or Community?*," in *A Testament of Hope: The Essential Writings and Speeches of Martin Luther King Jr.*, ed. James M. Washington (New York: Harper One, 1986), 562.

18. Lischer, *Preacher King*, 88–89.

19. Joseph Evans, *Lifting the Veil over Eurocentrism: The Du Boisian Hermeneutic of Double Consciousness* (Trenton, NJ: Africa World Press, 2014), 30–31.

20. Glaude, *Democracy in Black*, 6. The agency gap is similar to Glaude's value gap: "the belief that white people are valued more than others."

21. Evans, *Lifting the Veil*, 156.

22. Sallie McFague, *Metaphorical Theology: Models of God in Religious Language* (Philadelphia: Fortress, 1982), 17.

23. Lischer, *Preacher King*, 122.

24. Paul Ricoeur, *The Rule of Metaphor: Multi-disciplinary Studies of the Creation of Meaning in Language* (Toronto: University of Toronto Press, 1975), 9.

25. Kenneth Burke, *On Symbols and Society*, ed. Joseph Gusfield (Chicago: University of Chicago Press, 1989), 247.

26. McFague, *Metaphorical Theology*, 15.

27. Paul Ricoeur, *Interpretation Theory: Discourse and the Surplus of Meaning* (Fort Worth: Texas Christian University Press, 1976), 52.

28. King, "Pilgrimage to Nonviolence," 37.

29. W. E. B. Du Bois, *Dusk of Dawn: An Essay toward an Autobiography of a Race Concept* (Piscataway, NJ: Transaction, 2011), 47.

30. Lane Cooper, ed., *The Rhetoric of Aristotle* (London: Prentice-Hall, 1932), 185.

31. Ricoeur, *Rule of Metaphor*, 13.

32. Amanda Gorman, "The Hill We Climb: The Amanda Gorman Poem That Stole the Inauguration Show," The Guardian, January 20, 2021. See https://www.theguardian.com/us-news/2021/jan/20/amanda-gorman-poem-bideninauguration-transcript.

33. Cornel West, *Race Matters* (New York: Vintage, 2001), 19–20.

34. John McClure, *Other-wise Preaching: A Postmodern Ethic for Preaching* (Saint Louis: Chalice Press, 2001.

35. Cooper, *Rhetoric of Aristotle*, 199–200.

36. Ricoeur, *Rule of Metaphor*, 13.

37. Martin Luther King Jr., "The Summer of Our Discontent," in *Why We Can't Wait* (New York: Signet Classics, 2000), 146.

38. Cooper, *Rhetoric of Aristotle*, 9.

39. King, "Summer of Our Discontent," 133–34.

CHAPTER 3

How the Polished King Used Narrative and Rhetoric

> For the gifted young preacher, no less than the student of rhetoric, the effect of such a regimen was the supplantation of true spontaneity in public life by its premeditated affection. The preacher enjoyed freedom from the role only when he was away from the eye of congregation or in the unguarded company of his fellow preachers.[1]
> —Richard Lischer

We are familiar with the polished Martin Luther King Jr. His writings, sermons, and speeches are known and respected by a broad swath of the world's population. Before he experienced global recognition and reached his iconic status, he had to learn how to wax, buff, and shine what we know and understand to be the polished King's canon. I posit, then, that we have uncovered how King developed his polished narrative and rhetoric. In fact, I thought that in this chapter I would offer a singular guidepost for consideration of King's rhetoric. However, I have discovered that his narrative and rhetoric are nearly inseparable.

King's narrative grows from his and others' life experiences. His life was filled with encounters similar to that of Achilles and Odysseus in the *Iliad* and the *Odyssey*. This comparison points directly to his leadership role in the American civil rights movement (1955–68). As he attempted to explain to the American and international communities the daily occurrences of the movement, his narrative evolved and matured. Since his movement was *sui generis*, King must have recognized that an emergent rhetoric also grew from his narrative. I see this as necessary for King because it was his rhetoric that gave organization, arrangement, shape, and form to his narrative. Indeed, King's narrative is one of a kind, but it is his rhetoric that gives it continuing life. In this way, we begin to understand the polished King.

My motive for writing this book was to uncover King's polish. In fact, King's polish has not faded but has increased during the current globalized human crisis. It is as though he foreknew that worldwide, white tribalism and nationalism would come forth. As a response, King wove his own story line into a living narrative. His narrative chronicles his cohorts' and his own dream of Black liberation, which has inspired countless others. King understood that if his narrative would come to life, it would do so because of an adept use of living liberation rhetoric.

As we move forward, it is important for readers' comprehension that we address King's narrative and rhetoric as intersecting codependents. In short, one is dependent on the other. King's narrative and rhetoric, then, support how he wrote literature and preached the gospel. Both are responses against human oppression. We associate human oppression with hegemonic practices (i.e., white supremacy and white mythology). King's narrative and rhetoric bring hidden distractions and hegemonic practices to the surface.

King's narrative and rhetoric are examples of and justifications for our resistance against human oppression. Thus far I have written about his *living words*, a term I use interchangeably with *living metaphors*. Here I focus on his narrative and rhetoric. As indicated, I believe these are liberation motifs.

Thus, I believe that King employed these as supportive tools that intersect. Like a grapevine, the intersection is tightly interwoven. Any attempt to cut away a single strand of the grapevine risks unintended cutting of a strand or strands of the vine. My hope is that we are able to trace King's mastery over narrative and rhetoric and observe how each empowered him to face and confront hegemonic powers and structures.

Narrative and Its Components

We begin here with narrative, which one scholar defines in the following way:

> Narratives have the potential to explain *why* people act. . . . Narratives help give coherence and emotional resonance to events, resolving

> uncertainties and confusion for how to understand those events. Narratives provide "rationales for participation," and "stories also set the terms of strategic action [actions to be taken], defining what is an opportunity or an obstacle, a success or a failure, and a cost or a benefit."[2]

We grasp from this scholar a useful definition for narrative. It provides supportive evidence for why and how King created his liberation narrative. King's narrative informs his audiences, explains to his opponents, and attempts to depoliticize false claims but permits correct moral and ethical claims to be politicized.

King's narrative, then, does not completely depoliticize the civil rights movement. The oppressor's unsavory propaganda remains an unethical, immoral, deliberate politicization. Propagandistic politicization is used to this day to stoke visceral reactions against people who seek liberation from hegemonic practices. Consider cultural stakeholders and vanguards. You will notice their attempts to protect their socioeconomic and psychological privileges. You will locate distractions that are systematically developed, maintained, and intentionally designed and deployed to reinforce white mythologies among segments of the masses.

As in King's time, racism and economic, political, and psychological constructs stand between us and our shared emergent vision for our desired socio-human change. Like King, we are assigned to seek human transformation from our current culture, which continues to entangle us in webs of hegemonic injustices. These webs distract us from recognition of a realized democratic society. While we still yearn for a democratic society, we must continue to learn from King's use of narrative and rhetoric to set forth our demand for action. And action to be taken begins with all religious leaders.

Let us now fully claim that King's narrative is a liberation narrative. This is more exacting and describes that which Divinity reveals as actions to be taken. Divinity demands that, like King, we become chroniclers, assigned to explain to our readers, audiences, and congregations that which occurs in real time. In short, King the chronicler's narrative grows from the daily occurrences of the liberation movement:

> With narrative, the . . . innovation lies in the inventing of another work of synthesis—a plot, goals, causes, and chance are brought together within the temporal unity of a whole and complete action. It is this synthesis . . . that brings narrative close to metaphor. In both cases, the new thing—the as yet unsaid, the unwritten—springs up in language. Here a living metaphor, that is, a new pertinence in the prediction, there a feigned plot, that is, a new congruence in the organization of events.[3]

As Jacqueline Bacon writes, "Rhetors in a variety of contexts feature narration as persuasion, recognizing the rhetorical power of stories, metaphors, myths, gestures, and other means of creating communicative relationships."[4]

King's liberation narrative is organized and arranged with compelling plots, goals, causes, and chance, brought together within temporal unity, which I refer to as temporal qualities. I reemphasize that King's narrative demands that action be taken. And action to be taken is a pure and precise definition for rhetoric.

Also, King's living metaphors cause a new awareness and congruence of collective similarities and dissimilarities, which are often present in narrative organization and arrangement. Narrative and rhetoric are persuasive because of organization and arrangement. King was a master of persuasion, but that persuasion was underlined by his organization and arrangement of events and his living words that pointed toward a democratic society. For King and others, passion and persuasion can come with a cost that cannot be paid.

In most instances, we can speak robustly about how tragically but heroically King's life ended. King died fighting for a democratic society. This is true. However, it is truer that King died in defense of revealed truth. It is truest that all women and men are created equal by divine decree (Genesis 1:27; Matthew 19:12; Acts 8:36-37: Galatians 3:28). If we agree that we have clear evidence that humanity is equal, we also agree that the right to have a democratic society rises above all of this nation's secular documents. King defended that Divinity created all people as equals in the human family.

Nevertheless, King's life was taken by an assassin's bullet; however, his life continues through his liberation narrative because his rhetoric gives it life. This is what James Baldwin grasped. Baldwin understood King's liberation narrative and rhetoric and appreciated its organization and arrangement. More than that, Baldwin grasped that King's liberation narrative and rhetoric are eschatological and prophetic. It is more certain that Baldwin grasped that King was a master of living words. King bent words into word symbols to persuade us that there are plausible possibilities of a forthcoming democratic society.

Events as Story

King positioned his living words as metaphors within his liberation narrative to add shine. In other words, King's word symbols were strategically positioned to describe current events during the civil rights struggle. He understood that what made his narrative an attractive masterpiece was understanding the importance of creating temporal qualities. By temporal, I mean that King was a master of retelling civil rights events as a story that at some point comes to an end. Because there is an end, we recognize that we are reading or hearing a retelling of a story (this suggests that theoretically a narrative never ends). As alert readers of stories, narratives, and texts, we know to look for its embedded clues, what I refer to as satellites and kernels:

> All narratives include characters, settings, and plotlines. Characters serve many purposes in a [liberation] narrative; for example, they facilitate reader analysis for the narrative's content and substance. Settings are sometimes referred to as major events, and they must be called kernels; they also point readers toward characters in the setting. In addition, kernels are major events that suggest critical points in the narrative that force movement in particular directions. . . . Narratives also have minor plot events, which often involve developing characters. They are also referred to as satellites. . . . What is more, satellites do not have to appear in the immediate proximity of the kernels to which they are linked: they may appear anywhere in the narrative.[5]

Satellites and kernels then lead us to appreciate the whole of any story:

> A story . . . must be more than just an enumeration of events in serial order: it must organize them into an intelligible whole, of a sort that we can always ask what the "thought" of this story is. In short, emplotment [grasping characters, plot, scenes, and the role that this plays as we attempt to discern the distance between time and narrative] is the operation that draws a configuration [arrangement] out of a simple succession.[6]

Further,

> to follow a story is to move forward in the midst of contingencies . . . under the guidance of an expectation that finds its fulfillment in the "conclusion" of the story. This conclusion is not logically implied by the previous premise. It gives the story an "end point," which in turn, furnishes the point of view from which the story can be perceived as forming a whole. To understand the story is to understand how and why the successive episodes led to this conclusion, which, far from being foreseeable, must finally be acceptable, as congruent with the episodes brought together by the story.[7]

Readers immediately grasp that a brilliant story is underlined by its temporal qualities. King did not attempt to avoid historical accuracies. He did, however, try to help readers discern the significance of civil rights events, which he often linked to biblical texts.

The following is an example of King's understanding of a story's temporal qualities. While incarcerated in 1963, King wrote his "Letter from a Birmingham Jail." King reflected on recent events that caused fear among the Birmingham clergy, some of whom wrote an editorial in their local newspaper. The editorial's purpose was meant to denounce publicly King's presence and reasons for him being in Birmingham. These accusatory clergy were in opposition to King's Birmingham boycott and believed his reasons to be unfounded. The boycott was organized resistance against unjust local segregation laws. In his letter King presented evidence for his presence and protest in Birmingham; he had accepted an invitation from allies in the Black community.

King used his letter to reframe or retell a broader story about the purposes and actions that led to his incarceration. He underscored that state and local laws were unjust, unethical, immoral, and hegemonic. Below I focus on a particular part of the letter's text that supports my claim that a brilliant story has characters, plotlines, and temporal qualities:

> I have heard numerous southern religious leaders admonish their worshipers to comply with a desegregation decision because it is the law, but I have longed to hear white minsters declare: "Follow this decree because integration is morally right and because the Negro is your brother." In the midst of blatant injustices inflicted upon the Negro, I have watched white churchmen stand on the sideline and mouth pious irrelevancies and sanctimonious trivialities. In the midst of a mighty struggle to rid our nation of racial and economic injustice, I have heard many ministers say: "Those are social issues, with which the gospel has no real concern." And I have watched many churches commit themselves to a completely otherworldly religion which makes a strange, un-Biblical distinction between body and soul, between the sacred and the secular.[8]

King's brilliant use of similarities and dissimilarities dramatizes an "un-Biblical distinction between body and soul, between the sacred and the secular." However, the taproot of King's discourse is its temporal qualities. Although he did not neglect current events, he did blur historical linear lines. He accomplished this by positioning his accusatory local Birmingham clergy into a larger group of Southern clergies. He compared and contrasted the Birmingham clergy with those he had encountered across the American South: "I have heard numerous southern religious leaders admonish their worshipers to comply with a desegregation decision because it is the law."

In addition, the organization of King's narrative and rhetoric transforms the Birmingham clergy into a living metaphor to develop a broader plotline. His metaphor makes of his clergy a trope that serves as another form of a transformation process. He used his living trope to give voice to his movement's objective, which was to achieve complete integration both morally and economically. King then personified the Birmingham movement, which is another form of transformation process. This is brilliant storytelling. King's storytelling capacities were on full display as he used them to create rhetorical space to proclaim a way toward a new and hopeful (eschatological) future.

I see King's future as plausible and possible. In another layer of similarities and dissimilarities, the Birmingham clergy reinforced hegemonic practices while other Southern clergy whom King encountered complied with desegregation laws. The Birmingham clergy were villains. The other clergy were heroes and heroines. In biblical terms, the Birmingham clergy were accusers of the brothers and sisters (Revelation 12:10). This is apocalyptic language that announces that when God's salvation is revealed, there are demonic voices that accuse those who proclaim that salvation is God's.

King the grammarian transformed his accusative clergy into a living metaphor, a trope, and a word picture.[9] By accusative, I mean a grammatical verb form that identifies or points directly toward an object (commonly known as a direct object). The clergy, serving as a word picture, took on the form of an accusative verb. As a verb, they took action to make King their direct object of problems. Rather than engaging King, they refused to dialogue with him as Christians. Moreover, they attempted to demonize King. They refused to search for constructive answers that would lead to a plausible and possible future.

King's letter points to the apostle Paul: as Paul "left his village of Tarsus and carried the gospel of Jesus Christ to the far corners of the Greco-Roman world, so I am compelled to carry the gospel of freedom beyond my own hometown."[10] King the grammarian transformed the apostle Paul into a trope and word picture also. King compared and contrasted the apostle with himself. This reframing is meant to underscore similarities and dissimilarities. In this way King is reframed as a heroic figure. Again, this is an example of brilliant storytelling. Surely his accusers were proponents of Pauline theology, Paul's missionary journeys, and his cross-cultural Christian worldview. Adroitly, King created for his antagonists the plausible possibilities for an alternative narrative. King achieved this by his proper use of transformative and transformational word processes.

Transformative and Transformational Word Processes

King's word processes then point toward his alternative narrative that moves us beyond hegemonic interpretation of current events and biblical texts.

What is more, King resisted using biblical texts as reinforcement for white mythologies. Instead, King's word processes empowered him to deconstruct white mythologies. As a direct result, King created new space for his narrative and rhetoric to support his liberation motifs. He employed his motifs to defend equality of personhood and human worth. When these twin psychological and spiritual principles are defended, we find courage to face our unpredictable human realities. Thus, King carefully used his word processes to open doors. His alternative narrative makes us aware of new space and possibilities. Different narratives lead to transformative and transformational experiences. That is, transformative words and narratives speak to our awareness of differences in perceptions that shape our consciousness.

Another way to think of transformative words is by using a common rock or a millstone as a living metaphor. In a grinding mill, a millstone functions as a tool used to reduce hard substances into the simplest granular forms. The stone, then, as we use it, is a living metaphor. If we personify the millstone, we see it as individuals or as groups of persons. The grinding stone forces us to face heavy, inescapable, and burdensome responsibilities. A transformative quality is thus added to our living metaphor. King used his words similarly to create a transformative living metaphor:

> Never in American history had a group seized the streets, the squares, the sacrosanct business thoroughfares and the marbled halls of government to protest and proclaim the unendurability of their oppression. Had room-size machines turned human, burst from the plants that housed them and stalked the land in revolt, the nation could not have been more amazed. Undeniably, the Negro had been an object of sympathy and wore the scars of deep grievances, but the nation had come to count on him as a creature who could quietly endure, silently suffer and patiently wait. He was well trained in service and, whatever the provocation, he neither pushed back nor spoke back.[11]

King's living metaphor is powerful: "Had room-size machines turned human, burst from the plants that housed them and stalked the land in revolt, the nation could not have been more amazed." This is a proper use of transformative words that are meant to confront and force us to see grinding stones that reduce our human grievances to granular substances. The grinding millstone is symbolic of a process that is designed to make us face racial, gender, economic, political, and other human differences. In this instance, King confronted racism and forced oppressors to face the consequences of refusing to recognize and celebrate human differences.

Now we transition from words that are transformative to words that are transformational, or a word process that changes human consciousness. This process is never completed but continuously repeats (Romans 12:1-3). Words that are organized this way are catalysts for creating socio-human and socio-structural changes. If we follow King's adept use of word arrangements, we, too, can lead people toward organized efforts to change human conditions. Put differently, transformative words make us aware of spiritual and intellectual possibilities. They disrupt socio-human structures over time. Transformative and transformational words are manipulated and bent into new images.

Like transformative words, transformational words can be thought of as living metaphor, and here transformative words emerge as a milestone. A milestone is a physical stone used as a marker to indicate distance traveled. King crafted a living metaphor of a milestone and arranged it so his readers could visualize the frustration of Negro people. In this way, King demonstrated that he not only understood the frustrations of Negro people but also shared their woeful experiences. The priestly King is called to serve as our liberator. We see, then, that the milestone marks distance that oppressed people continue to travel. King was arguing that they had traveled far enough, and that oppressed people were no longer pacified with gradual progress. King was emphasizing the urgency of now.

King's effort to bring liberation to life is like a living metaphor of a milestone that he employed to highlight contrasts and comparisons. He acknowledged slow progress and the unacceptable time it took to travel from one milestone to another. This dramatized the justifiable collective frustration of the Negro people over oppressors taking their time to change hegemonic practices that reduced the human worth of the oppressed.

King's living metaphor, then, was a response that affirmed justifiable Negro social protest. Negroes were resisting white hegemonic power structures that were deliberately delaying positive action:

> The Negro has been deeply disappointed over the slow pace of school desegregation. He knew that in 1954 the highest court in the land had handed down a decree calling for desegregation of schools "with all deliberate speed." He knew that this edict from the Supreme Court had been heeded with all deliberate delay. At the beginning of 1963, nine years after this historic decision, approximately 9 percent of southern Negro students were attending integrated schools. If this pace were maintained, it would be the year of 2054 before integration in southern schools would be a reality.[12]

King called the United States Supreme Court decision a "decree and edict" and resisted calling the decision a justifiable ratified law. He resisted the latter because the decisions of the highest court of the land are supposed to be enacted and reinforced by all federal, state, and local jurisdictions. King's living metaphor is made visible by his use of juxtaposition. King wrote that the court had called for "desegregation of schools 'with all deliberate speed.'" Instead, the decree had been "heeded with all deliberate delay."

King had to learn how to bend his words to give them new life. This is what I mean by transformative and transformational words. King's words are catalysts for change. Moreover, King's words become new objects of persuasion. Words bent in new ways create living words or living metaphors. Once again, these catalytic words help to reveal unforeseen plausible possibilities. King's successful manipulation of words is used to demand action to be taken. This is the primary role and function of rhetoric, to which we now turn.

Rhetoric

Rhetoric is the art and science of persuasion. In a broader sense, rhetoric has rudimentary rules that we continue to learn through its classical forms and traditions.[13] King was exposed to these rules as a teenager in his educational process. His first tutor, Gladstone Louis Chandler, was known as an institutional pillar of the venerable Morehouse College. Chandler was like a drill sergeant, one scholar claims: the "rigor of his speech course was a tradition his recruits both dreaded and enjoyed."[14] Before he taught King, in a similar way Chandler taught Martin Luther King Sr. Chandler's primary text was the *Fundamentals of Public Speaking*.[15] This text was widely respected and broadly utilized by rhetoricians to teach both novice and advanced students the depths of rhetoric.

Donald Cross Bryant and Karl Richard Wallace, editors of this important volume, included historic and significant speeches, evidence of rhetoric's value to the literary canon of Western civilization. They contributed chapters on pedagogy and other subjects that increase the polish of their students of rhetoric. Below I present two excerpts from the volume, which I believe provide a window into King's rhetorical mind:

> As the study of public speaking has enjoyed the dignity and importance in all the ages of Western civilization, so it is important today when the demands upon the spoken word and the facilities for transmitting it are so much greater than ever before. Today, of course, in the running of our complicated society, we have the additional aid of tremendous qualities of all sorts of printed matter. But because of the extent and increased complexity of our social, economic, and political life, there is not less but more demand for oral communication. . . . The student will want to recognize the values which modern society associates with public speaking. Some are personal; some are social. Some are self-evident, because they are linked to such motives as self-improvement, personal success, and confidence. Others are less evident, because they are connected with such values as social responsibility and welfare of others.[16]

What Bryant and Wallace call public speaking can also be understood as rhetoric in oral performance. It is significant that their focus is primarily on the rhetoric of consequential orators. The Western rhetorical tradition, according to these writers, suggests that rhetoric is important for communication in a demanding society. What is more, they place emphasis on "social responsibility and welfare of others."

Rhetoric and Democracy

Rhetoric is used to advocate for democracy, and when rhetoric is organized properly as an argument in the hands of a skillful rhetor, it can aid a rhetor's defense against false propagandistic claims. Rhetoric then is egalitarian. It is a democratic act. Rhetoric gives social life: "Democracy is a way of social life in which ultimate power and responsibility reside in the people and are shared by them. To share power and responsibility is to believe that all men [and women] are competent to understand the goal and methods of representative government and are capable of learning its skills and of taking part effectively in its process."[17]

In addition, "a democratic society makes two assumptions which bear critically upon communication. First is the assumption that democracy will not work unless there is general communication among men [and women]—a constant and effective interchange of both fact and opinion." Moreover, another principle of a "democratic society is that if communication is widespread and free, knowledge will prevail over ignorance, and truth will win over falsehood."[18]

It appears that in addition to understanding the rudiments of rhetoric, the polished King understood the rudiments of democracy, which include a firm grasp on how rhetoric functions at the center of Western civilization and has a role in defending democracy against hegemonic practices. It has an equally important role in shaping public opinion and persuading and is thus useful for facilitating debate among informed citizens, especially in defending truth over falsehood.

"The Other America" is among the most significant public addresses in King's canon. An excerpt from this address demonstrates King's grasp of Bryant and Wallace's belief that Western civilization has attached itself to democracy and its orators. King, as a Christian orator, understood that he had a responsibility to bring forth truth over falsehood.

> I'd like to use as a subject from which to speak this afternoon, the other America. And I use this subject because there are literally two Americas. One America is beautiful for our situation. And in a sense, this America is overflowing with the miracle of prosperity and the honey of opportunity. This America is the habitat of millions of people who have food and material necessities for their bodies and culture and education for their minds, and freedom and human dignity for their spirit. In this America, millions of people

> experience every day the opportunity of having life, liberty, and the pursuit of happiness in all of their dimensions. And in this America, millions of young people grow up in the sunlight of opportunity.[19]

In two minutes and ten seconds, King uttered 126 words, of which 7.5 percent were the word *America*. King created a chain stitch, a pattern to reinforce his theme. The phrase "two Americas" is living words and here a euphemism. King employed this phrase to underscore that two socioeconomic and sociopsychological segregated systems exist, function, and are legally sanctioned ("America is beautiful for our situation").

King alluded to an Old Testament passage that promises a realized democratic and fair society for the socio-marginalized and the abject impoverished and oppressed. The promise is that the Hebrew people were to be equal citizens who shared with others the resources of a democratic land "overflowing with the miracle of prosperity and the honey of opportunity." King's statement paralleled Yahweh's promise to the enslaved Hebrew people: "I have come down to deliver them from the Egyptians, and to bring them up out of that land to a good and broad land, a land flowing with milk and honey" (Exodus 3:8).

"The Other America" demonstrates that King was an unrivaled orator but also that he was a brilliant storyteller. We know that King began his speech with his characterization of America's propositions, but he finished with an adroit addition. American democracy depends on an agreed-upon social order, and it survives when its citizens are civic-minded and skillful and know truth over falsehood. According to King, democracy depends on faith. It is faith that prefers truth over false claims. Faith is necessary to sustain democracy. It is faith, then, that is invoked in order to believe the obvious, that all people are created equal in the sight of Divinity and humanity:

> I say that if the inexpressible cruelties of slavery couldn't stop us, the opposition that we now face, including the so-called white backlash, will surely fail. We're going to win our freedom. Because both the sacred heritage of our nation and the will of the Almighty God are embodied in our echoing demands. And so, I can still sing we shall overcome. We shall overcome because somehow the arc of

> the universe is long, but it bends toward justice. We shall overcome because Carlisle is right. No lie can live forever. We shall overcome because William Cullen Bryant is right. Truth crushed to earth will rise again. We shall overcome because James Russell Lowell is right. Truth is forever on the scaffold wronged, forever on the throne. Yet the scaffold sways the future. With this faith we will be able to hew out of the mountain of despair, a stone of hope, this faith. We will be able to transform the jangling discords of our nation into a beautiful symphony of brotherhood [and sisterhood].
>
> With this faith, we will be able to speed up the day when all of God's children, Black men [and women], white men [and women], Jews and Gentiles, Protestants and Catholics, will be able to join hands and live together as brothers [and sisters], all over this great nation. That will be a great day. That will be a great tomorrow. In the word sure to speak symbolically, that will be the day when the morning stars will sing together, and the sons [and daughters] of God will shout for joy [Job 38:7]. Thank you.[20]

King was an excellent orator on the public platform. After he made his demand that action be taken by his audience, he passionately reinforced the claims of his argument. The conclusion of his speech was that of a Baptist preacher who by faith peered through the veil and appealed to Divinity to justify his case. In addition, King's oratory demonstrates that there is an intersection between democracy and rhetoric.

There is no doubt that Chandler had a similar appreciation for the utilities of rhetoric. He must have taught its vital role, which is to preserve and protect a free and democratic society. It is plausible, then, that Chandler instilled the rhetorical principles of Bryant and Wallace in his recruits and particularly in King. A part of Chandler's understanding would include the following:

> Rhetoric in Greece was specifically the civic art of public speaking as it developed under constitutional government, especially in Athenian democracy of the fifth and fourth centuries. The art was described and discussed in handbooks, speeches, dialogues, trea-

> tises, and lectures and was expanded and developed by teachers of public speaking, philosophers, and practicing orators to produce what we call "classical rhetoric," social and political practices and a body of texts that describe or illustrate that practice. Classical rhetoric, in turn, was transmitted to the Middle Ages, the Renaissance and the modern period, adapted to the needs of each era, but repeatedly drawing new inspiration from the major classical sources, especially from writings of Cicero, but at times from readings of Plato, Aristotle, Quintilian, or other Greek or Latin sources.[21]

As indicated earlier, the Kings were taught these classical forms of rhetoric, in addition to rudimentary pedagogies found in Bryant and Wallace. What is of import here is that we can attach desires for democracy to the younger King and the rhetoric he employed as a means to achieve democracy in America. Rhetoric was birthed from yearnings for human equality. Without human equality, the reality of a democratic society will continue to elude us.

For King, American values and principles were on trial. King demanded that America and his audience were to act according to the evidence he had placed before them.

Rhetoric and Human Spectacle

On the public platform and behind the sacred desk, King was a persuasive rhetor. Moreover, he grasped that people are attracted to human spectacle. It was said about Frederick Douglass that he personified the human spectacle. Each time Douglass stood and addressed biased skeptics, they were fascinated if not obsessed with his body, voice, and words. They were attracted to his body and curious about how he survived bondage. What they saw was his courage to face his ordeal and become a premier abolitionist leader in the human rights struggle. One writer labeled him as a man caught up into "Black stardom," described in contemporary reports as "a Negro Hercules." She also noted that audiences in the 1840s were obsessed with the male Black body, hence the fascination with Douglass.[22]

Perhaps in this instance "Negro Hercules" is an appropriate metaphor for Black bodies, male and female, in authorial performances not related to entertainment (i.e., actors, singers, and sports figures). According to another scholar, the authorial Black body is not a new phenomenon. In fact, since the American antebellum period, the Black human body has been considered a spectacle:

> For African American orators who spoke before predominately white or biracial audiences, the process of claiming the authority to name racial difference took on an added significance. Their presence on the platform would evoke for antebellum audiences the connotations of physical difference, particularly the claims that such distinctions were proof of inferiority. The reports of Douglass's lectures, for example, frequently refer to his body quite explicitly, revealing as Robert Fanuzzi notes, that white audiences considered "the physique of the Black orator" a public spectacle.[23]

King would have been aware that he was thought of as a spectacle. He took full advantage, however, knowing that his body was an obsession for white audiences, both proponents and antagonists. King's awareness of this was not a new phenomenon. I imagine he considered his status as a spectacle each time he addressed an audience and congregation.

An obvious example of King's authorial Black body was on display during his iconic "I Have a Dream" civic sermon, which he delivered on August 28, 1963. I remember the sociopolitical context and the sea of faces aligned around the reflecting pool in the nation's capital. King stood before throngs of expectant people in his customary black suit, tie, and white shirt, and he delivered a message organized, arranged, informed, and shaped by his liberation narrative and rhetoric.

I focus here on King's claim that action must be taken for Negroes to receive economic reparations, and I take notice of the symbolism associated with the Lincoln Memorial:

> The 1963 March on Washington gathered in front of the Lincoln Memorial in order to connect symbolically the goals of the Civil Rights Movement with Abraham Lincoln's emancipation of the slaves. The result was to transform forever the meaning of the Washington Mall, which is now widely understood as a place where

> aggrieved populations can gather to register their discontent with social, economic, or political conditions.[24]

In this setting King proclaimed,

> So, we've come here today to dramatize a shameful condition. In a sense we've come to our nation's capital to cash a check. When the architects of our republic wrote the magnificent words of the Constitution and the Declaration of Independence, they were signing a promissory note to which every American was to fall heir. This note was a promise that all men [and women], yes, Black men [and women] as well as white men [and women], would be guaranteed the unalienable rights of life, liberty, and the pursuit of happiness.[25]

Because King was positioned before the Lincoln Memorial, immediately we note the contrasting symbolism between King's and Lincoln's narratives. (King became a visual rhetor, a concept I will address later.) Therein lies the justification for King sharing the Negro's narrative, a narrative that represents those who suffer and share their forebears' human oppression.

In addition, King was Douglass-like, a human spectacle. King the spectacle lifted his sonorous voice, and it came forth from his Black male body. His voice and body were in performance and on full display. King was aware that he was a part of a long but tawdry tradition of a stereotypical phenomenon.

Another glaring example of what it means to be gawked at as a human spectacle can be found in the biblical book of Acts. The writer, Luke, created a portrait of a persuasive rhetor standing in the public square proclaiming peculiar claims of a deity. What followed were skeptical reactions to those peculiar claims: "Some Epicurean and Stoic philosophers debated with him [the apostle Paul]. Some said, 'What does this babbler want to say?' Others said, 'He seems to be a proclaimer of foreign divinities.' (This was because he was telling the good news of Jesus and the resurrection)" (Acts 17:18).

Nothing is more attractive than an eloquent speaker delivering an eloquent public speech. The speech or religious discourse is transformative when it is uttered uniquely during peculiar times. By peculiar, I mean awkward and uncomfortable circumstances that influence rhetorical conditions.

King was like a millstone that crushes hard and complex materials into smaller granular substances. His rhetoric was effective precisely because it was delivered during an uncomfortable time to the establishment and the status quos. Further, because of King's life-giving rhetorical arrangement of his narrative, it continued to speak hauntingly long after the sea of faces disappeared into the day and long after King left the platform. In fact, King's recordings and letters are heard and read to this day. This longevity adds to our understanding of transformational words. Still, it is important that we underscore that King came to rhetorical prominence during a period of awkward uncertainty (1955–68).

Often King's narrative and rhetoric parallel motifs of biblical justice. Biblical narratives such as that of the exodus express our universal human and spiritual yearning for democratic principles (Exodus 7:1-4). Indeed, King's narrative and rhetoric are examples for preachers and other orators who want to effectively create characters and plotlines, kernels and satellites, transformative, transformational, and living words, and word pictures. I have provided examples and evidence that these are located in biblical texts to influence how strategically we plan for democratic institutional change.

The Interplay of Narrative and Rhetoric

King's rhetoric gives life to his story. His rhetoric captures human action as it occurs in real time. By human action, I mean action to be taken. For example, King compels us to become his congregants who listen to his sermons. During the crucifixion scene, the writer of Matthew's gospel describes a haunting occurrence. The writer reports that people who were believed to be dead walked around Jerusalem. At the same time, and near the place of Jesus' crucifixion, an earthquake occurred and other strange things. The writer goes on to say, that a Roman soldier (centurion) was persuaded that Jesus "truly this was the Son of God" (Matthew 27:54). This serves as a segue. During King's involvement in the civil rights struggles, the ghostly King's voice and actions haunt America's conscious and persuade some to accept King's passionate appeal for democratic justice and truth. Through his voice that lifts from his Black male body, he has grabbed our attention by weaving his biblical text, sermon topic, and current affairs to create a chain stitch. The stitch is a part of his liberation narrative. Here we are focused on his rhetoric, which gives life to his story. We remember that rhetoric adds form to oral and written discourses.

Now imagine that we are following King to lecture halls of influential universities and colleges, where we observe the intensity levels rising as we observe truth and spirituality colliding. As King speaks, we feel his words entering into our secret places. We cannot deny it; his words demand that we act. Words that are arranged in a proper fashion persuade and demand that action be taken. When we accept the charge and embrace leadership roles inside movements that will change our generation, the orator or writer gains confidence that we want to participate in her or his noble causes.

When we read King's literature, we sense that his living words have a throbbing heart. Stricken by silence while trying to trace his thoughts, we even attempt to anticipate the direction we are to travel with him. We ponder his living words, the depth of his narrative, and the form of his composition. Because of his polish, we make a personal and silent commitment that becomes a bodily act of faith. We are determined to meet him at his final destination. We begin to bear witness to his just and noble cause. Like James Baldwin, we have been persuaded that action is to be taken. This is the polished King.

Furthermore, like Baldwin, we are called to become King's allies, and with him we march into unavoidable trials and tribulations that come as a result of our decision to share in his human protest movement. The human protest movement forms an organic narrative. It is rhetoric, however, that gives life to the narrative, because rhetoric persuades people to embrace a higher plane of moral and ethical consciousness. King thus depended on his rhetoric to shape a new consciousness in those who enter into his narrative. If we enter into his narrative, we have entered into King's protest movement; we have entered into a struggle for human rights and justice.

We react this way because the narrative has been arranged in such a way as to be persuasive. Rhetoric composes, organizes, and arranges narrative, including writings, sermons, and speeches. King's rhetoric, then, is composition—form, shape, organization, and arrangement of thoughts. King's rhetoric persuades that action be taken because he has organized and arranged our thoughts to trace his thoughts like we are walking on a train track. If we stay on the rails, eventually we will arrive at our destination. We can visualize how audiences find themselves emotionally involved with King's narrative and rhetoric. Some of them are sympathetic with King's positions, for achieving human rights via the civil rights movement.

Not only does King's rhetoric attract sympathetic interpreters of the narrative, but it also attracts courageous enlistees and like-minded allies. It is used to persuade audiences to listen to the narrative. As a result, we become coparticipants in the human rights struggle. In short, attracted by his rhetoric, we become a part of King's living human protest narrative. We grasp that a narrative can be ahistorical, that it continues as needed. We know that the struggle to realize equality continues in our time and space.

King's narrative suspends chronological time like an ahistorical narrative that appears in the New Testament and has meaning beyond chronological time. This is *kairos* time—time that belongs solely to Divinity's grace. This is a theological motif. This is rhetoric.

Rhetoric gives life to narrative, and King's persuasive rhetoric attracts us to come alongside others in the movement. Even now as we read about the civil rights era, we are attracted to his narrative because his rhetoric gives it life. And the life of King's narrative continues in our current human struggles because our human struggles continue to be unresolved. Regrettably, we continue to struggle with universal recognition of our human equality, personhood, and worth.

In the struggle, we recognize our own faces. We understand and acknowledge how we feel. We sense our unexpected courage in the face of imminent danger. Still, we march. We march into jail cells. We march until we are tired and smell of fear. We march as emotional and moral agents against intimidating hegemonic practices that are designed to overtake our newfound courage. But our protest is just. King created rhetoric that shapes his liberation narrative, causing it to read like we are watching a network's evening news reports—and we see ourselves on our television screens. King's rhetoric masterfully underlines and supports his masterful narrative.

I have deliberately made repetitive statements that claim rhetoric gives life to any narrative. I have done so to create a chain stitch meant to be a living metaphor that points to a thematic pattern. The pattern then points to what we shall see as a living narrative and rhetoric in performance. King's narrative and rhetoric come to life because humans participate in social protests that are necessary to bear truth over falsehood against hegemonic power. This is the taproot of all human justice movements.

My pattern parallels what Ezekiel experienced in the valley of dry bones. The bones lived because of the Spirit of Divinity is infused into an oppressed people. The writer makes clear, "I will put my spirit within you, and you shall live" (Ezekiel 37:14). This stands near to my claim of the function of rhetoric, namely, rhetoric is like the role of *ruach* (breath or spirit; the Spirit) over the armies in the valley of dry bones and breathes life into the narrative (see also Psalm 51:9-10). In a similar way, rhetoric adds life to the narrative. Otherwise, the narrative is too dry—if it is not dead. King's narrative would have died, but people grasped that it was their narrative as well as King's.

Earlier in this chapter, I claimed that King's narrative as well as his rhetoric grew from his and others' life experiences. I also made a claim that rhetoric breathed life into King's narrative. The narrative is one and the same with the civil rights movement's social justice protests. There was no one who understood this more than Wyatt Tee Walker, who served as King's chief of staff and architect of the Birmingham boycott.

Walker organized the strategies that transformed King's narrative and rhetoric into a living, breathing body and soul and eventually into a standing army. The army stood in the middle of the Birmingham valley of dry bones. Once again, this occurred in real time and space. Without Walker, we may never have seen the victories that we associate with King's civil rights epoch, which are similar to the victories of Achilles and Odysseus.

One writer describes Walker as "a riveting preacher . . . [who] was brilliant, domineering, and egocentric, having ruled and lifted the SCLC [Southern Christian Leadership Conference] during its glory run."[26] In contrast, however, it is important for readers to read Walker's impressions of and relationship with King in his own words:

> The "Letter from a Birmingham Jail" was prompted by local clergymen, a rabbi, and a Black minister who said that this was not the time for protest action. Dr. King reacted to it. He was in jail, and his lawyers brought out his comments on the edge of newspapers and toilet paper and whatever paper they could provide him with.

> . . . I was the only one in Birmingham who could understand and translate Dr. King's chicken-scratch writing. So, I translated it. Quakers, or Friends Committee, wanted to call it "Tears of Love," and I told them no. It needed to be called what it was, a letter from a Birmingham jail. My personal secretary, Willie Pearl Mackey, sat on a typewriter while I translated it, and she typed it. . . . She was exhausted. . . . Because I could type, I finished the translation. And then we had to send it back to Dr. King to make sure he was satisfied with it. . . . So that's the story of the "Letter from a Birmingham Jail," which I think is the most important document of the twentieth century.[27]

Walker is a historic figure if for no other reason than that he is responsible for the translation and completion of the "Letter from a Birmingham Jail" and its eventual publication and worldwide distribution. He was brilliant and confident in his abilities to organize and execute plans that birthed a new consciousness and a new sociohistorical paradigm. As scholar Gary Dorrien indicated, we may call Walker egocentric. Nevertheless, it is unrealistic to suggest that a person lacking Walker's superego could perform such heroic feats under pressure as Walker proved he could do. Walker was courageous, and he was invested intellectually and spiritually in the movement. More importantly, Walker was invested in his relationship with Martin Luther King Jr. Walker described their relationship:

> Both of us are legitimate heirs of the African American free church; both of us of are sons of preachers; our God-given intellects were honed by the discipline of completing earned doctorates; our nonviolent credo was fashioned in the classrooms of the academy but also in the trenches of the Egyptian land of the Deep South; both of us have created a credible body of published works; and the center of our being is a personal commitment to Jesus Christ as Savior and Liberator. The uniqueness of these similarities provides an opportunity that so far as I know has not been seized by any of our contemporaries of our common struggle.[28]

Walker made clear that King needed gifted and committed people around him who philosophically and spiritually supported the movement. There is minimal space to suggest that without Walker's commitment to the "common struggle," as Walker characterized it, King's narrative and rhetoric would have become a living, breathing body and soul, and a standing army. What Walker achieved, we now think of as creating a visual narrative and rhetoric.

The Birmingham boycott has been romanticized by passing of time. People have gone to great lengths to revise and reposition their involvement in the movement and allege that they were on the right side of history. However, in real time, this was not the position taken by most persons. In this instance, during the Birmingham boycott, Walker struggled initially to create positive support from Black and white media outlets. Media labeled King as an outsider. This notion was a subject King addressed in the letter. Walker and King struggled to enlist volunteers. According to one scholar, "King thought he had 250 volunteers ready to get arrested, but only 70 showed up."[29]

In addition, Walker, who was dispatched to Birmingham in advance, found it difficult to enlist Black preachers to support resistance against Jane and Jim Crow segregation laws. There was infighting among Black public figures, some jostling for undue credit. For some, public recognition would have been problematic for the credibility of the movement.

Theophilus Eugene ("Bull") Connor, then commissioner of public safety in Birmingham, was the boycott's incendiary white supremacist in residence, the boycott's most formidable, albeit flawed, foe. Connor was eager to uphold Birmingham's hegemonic laws and practices. He was impetuous, and he craved attention. His narcissism controlled him, and like the biblical character Belshazzar, he could not interpret the handwriting on the wall (Daniel 5:1-9). Connor's lust for power and attention made him appear drunk on the wine of this world. His lack of control over his impulses led to egoistical mistakes that seemed providential more than coincidental.

In the meantime, it was clear that many Birmingham adults were afraid to be arrested by the Birmingham police. To oppose white hegemonic practices would cost them legally and economically. Because of their fear, the movement needed to enlist children in active roles, including participating in protest marches. Indeed, the children were heroes and heroines: "Tomorrow [the] students are gonna show you old folks what you should have done forty years ago. They're gonna make you ashamed to see that they have to go through what you should have gone through earlier for them, to, make their life better, said Walker."[30]

Walker knew that Conner's ego would lead to his political and strategic mistakes. Walker recalled,

> Birmingham would have been lost if Bull had let us go down to the City Hall and pray; if he had let us do that and stepped aside, what else would be new? There would be no movement, no publicity. But all he could see was stopping us before we got there. We had calculated for the stupidity of Bull Connor. He was a perfect adversary, Connor wanted publicity, he wanted his name in the paper. He believed that he would be the state's most popular politician if he treated the Black violently, bloodily, and sternly. We knew that the psyche of the white redneck was such that he would inevitably do something to help our cause.[31]

Because of Walker's strategic organization of King's written narrative and rhetoric, it was transformed into a visual narrative, and rhetoric for visual performance. This is a living metaphor. A word symbol here is identified as a living army that participates in the protest marches. The army was Spirit-filled children who were marching, protesting, and being jailed. This is a living metaphor that symbolizes that a breathing and living body with a spiritual soul can form an army and resist hegemonic practices. In short, the people were a living rhetoric, which is persuasive action to be taken.

The Birmingham boycott was televised nationally and internationally. Predominately the boycott was experienced through Black-and-white videos and photographs. Audiences were horrified by pictures and live video of unmerciful police brutality. State and local public safety officers regularly turned fire hoses and loosed biting police dogs onto children. The American culture of violence and death was on display. The culture was uncovered by sit-ins, Negroes' refusal to use public transportation, and their refusal to patronize downtown stores owned by citizens of the dominating classes of Birmingham's hegemonic culture. In short, Birmingham became a visual representation of the American culture of violence and death. Photos and videos documented an undemocratic people who refused to become a breathing social democracy.

The boycott then is representation of a visual art and science of persuasion, a demand for action to be taken. What Walker organized and arranged is referred to as visual rhetoric or video activism,

> or symbolic actions enacted primarily through visual means. Images help us to understand the world around us and form opinions and develop attitudes. Visuals have considerable persuasive power [rhetoric], being less intrusive than words and able to evoke strong emotional responses. Protest is intrinsically emotive, especially for, but not only with respect to, those protesting. In the context of protest, emotional imagery is used in order to influence and affect an audience's perspective in a favorable way and to elicit and develop empathy. Such uses of images, symbols, and places provide examples of ingenious ways in which activists appropriate new communication technologies in order to extend their action repertoire and achieve the goals associated with their struggles.[32]

The Birmingham boycott was a forerunner and representation of contemporary media communication. Walker carefully staged the protest marches in time to be included in the evening news. Media coverage of Birmingham's cruelties made the town appear to be the infamous center of the universe. Not only did Walker arrange these episodes for television and print media, but he also used the black-and-white still photographs to provoke the profound socio-human change the boycott sought. Those photos continue to be seen around the world more than fifty-eight years later. The images continue to haunt our past and present and inform our future.

Walker's visual rhetoric was arranged to shape the composition of King's narrative. Rhetoric makes the narrative persuasive and demands that action be taken. Visual rhetoric aims to produce emotional imagery. If people become sympathetic to the protest of the oppressed, this creates for their movement enduring images and symbols. The images and symbols or living metaphors help to create the movement's ethos credibility. What is more, people who empathize with protestors are moral agents who demonstrate solidarity, even if it is passively neutral solidarity. Because of the protest, the neutral moral agents discover they share similar values and beliefs with the protestors. Because of visual rhetoric, people are motivated to coparticipate as resisters against unjust laws and hegemonic practices.

Martin Luther King's and Wyatt Tee Walker's oral, written, and visual narrative and rhetoric bring the narrative to life. We will continue this discussion in the next chapter, but the Birmingham boycott is more than a symbol. It is a religious experience, and I suggest it is an incarnational episode similar to "And the Word became flesh and dwelt among us, and we have seen his glory, glory as of the only Son from the Father, full of grace and truth" (John 1:14, ESV). The Word of God (the Old and New Testaments) lifts from the pages of parchments. The Birmingham boycott is continuing revelatory words that are proclaimed by biblical prophets. The boycott is like other words recited by priests in liturgies and like the hymns and psalms that are sung by church choirs, which is another kind of recital of Divinity's Word. This is incarnation. Nevertheless, King's narrative is incomplete and quite possibly likely to die if action is not taken toward engaging in human rights struggles. Without the Spirit and the Word married together, the narrative becomes dry and lifeless. It needs a rhetoric or the Holy Spirit to come into the world and bring the narrative to life. The biblical incarnation of Word and Spirit are inseparable. King's narrative and rhetoric are nearly inseparable, as evidenced in the Birmingham boycott.

Of course, those who participated in the civil rights struggles were not perfect. However, the civil rights movement narrative demonstrates similarities to biblical texts. This is difficult to deny and to contemplate, if not see or admit. King's narrative and rhetoric follow similar lines as John's claim: "And the Word became flesh." The Word or the narrative became a living, breathing person with a complete anatomical and physiological system. Divinity then became human. Metaphorically, then, King's movement is a species of incarnation. King's incarnation is attached to the civil rights movement and social protests. This living narrative composed, organized, and arranged by his rhetoric keeps King rhetorically alive.

Notes

1. Richard Lischer, *Martin Luther King Jr. and the Word That Moved America* (Oxford: Oxford University Press, 1995), 41.

2. Amy Pason, "Strategic Storytelling: 'Our Home' Narratives of Occupy Home," in *The Rhetoric of Social Movements: Networks, Power, and New Media*, ed. Nathan Crick (New

York: Routledge, 2021), 85–86.

3. Paul Ricoeur, *Time and Narrative*, vol. 1 (Chicago: University of Chicago Press, 1983), ix.

4. Jaqueline Bacon, *The Humblest May Stand Forth: Rhetoric, Empowerment, and Abolition* (Columbia: University of South Carolina Press, 2002), 60.

5. Joseph Evans, *Lifting the Veil over Eurocentrism: The Du Boisian Hermeneutic of Double Consciousness* (Trenton, NJ: Africa World Press, 2014), 161–62.

6. Ricoeur, *Time and Narrative*, 65.

7. Ricoeur, 66.

8. Martin Luther King Jr., "Letter from a Birmingham Jail," in *Why We Can't Wait* (New York: Signet Classics, 2000), 105.

9. Henry Louis Gates Jr., *The Signifying Monkey: A Theory of African American Literary Criticism* (Oxford: Oxford University Press, 1988), 56–57.

10.Martin Luther King Jr., quoted in Gates, 86.

11. Martin Luther King Jr., *Why We Can't Wait* (New York: Signet Classics, 2000), 2.

12. King, *Why We Can't Wait*, 5.

13. Lischer, *Martin Luther King Jr.*, 41.

14. Lischer, 41.

15. Donald Cross Bryant and Karl Richard Wallace, *Fundamentals of Public Speaking* (New York: Meredith, 1947).

16. Bryant and Wallace, 5.

17. Bryant and Wallace, 7.

18. Bryant and Wallace, 8.

19. Martin Luther King Jr., "The Other America," in *The Radical King*, ed. Cornel West (Boston: Beacon, 2015), 235–44. The speech was delivered on March 10, 1968, in New York City. King was there in support of an effort to mobilize a multiracial movement of the poor. The event was organized by the Local 1199, "a union consisting largely of African Americans, Puerto Ricans, and other people of color" (235).

20. Martin Luther King Jr., "The Other America Speech Transcript—Martin Luther King Jr." Rev, accessed July 6, 2021, https://www.rev.com/blog/transcripts/the-other-america-speech-transcript-martin-luther-king-jr. This version of "The Other America" was delivered at Stanford University on April 14, 1967.

21. George A. Kennedy, *Classical Rhetoric and Its Christian and Secular Tradition from Ancient to Modern Times* (Chapel Hill: University of North Carolina Press, 1999), 1.

22. Hannah Rose Murray, "A 'Negro Hercules': Frederick Douglass' Celebrity in Britain," in *Celebrity Studies* 7, no. 2 (2016): 264–79.

23. Bacon, *Humblest May Stand Forth*, 73. See also Joseph Evans, *The Art of Eloquence: The Sacred Rhetoric of Gardner C. Taylor* (Valley Forge, PA: Judson, 2020), 154.

24. Charles E. Morris III and Stephen Howard Browne, *Readings on the Rhetoric of Social Protest* (State College, PA: Strata, 2001), 246.

25. Martin Luther King Jr., "I Have a Dream," in *A Testament of Hope: The Essential Writings and Speeches of Martin Luther King Jr.*, ed. James M. Washington (New York: HarperOne, 1986), 217–20.

26. Gary Dorrien, *Breaking White Supremacy: Martin Luther King Jr. and the Black Social Gospel* (New Haven, CT: Yale University Press, 2018), 241.

27. Wyatt Tee Walker, quoted in Evans, *Reconciliation and Reparation* (Valley Forge, PA: Judson Press, 2018), 35–36.

28. Wyatt Tee Walker, quoted in Evans, *Reconciliation and Reparation*, 36–37.

29. Dorrien, *Breaking White Supremacy*, 322.

30. Wyatt Tee Walker, quoted in Dorrien, 337.

31. Walker, quoted in Dorrien, 338.

32. Anastasia Veneti and Stamatis Poulakidakos, "Video-Activism and Small-Scale Resistance," in *The Rhetoric of Social Movements: Networks, Power, and New Media*, ed. Nathan Crick (New York: Routledge, 2021), 68–69.

CHAPTER 4

The Polished King Conceived a New Theology

> At that moment, I experienced the presence of the Divine as I had never before experienced. . . . It seemed as though I could hear the quiet assurance of an inner voice, saying, "Stand up for righteousness, stand up for truth. God will be at your side forever." Almost at once my fears began to pass from me. My uncertainty disappeared. I was ready to face anything. The outer situation remained the same, but God had given me inner calm.
> —Martin Luther King Jr.[1]

Triggered by an uncomfortable confluence of events, Martin Luther King Jr. experienced an existential crisis. As the civil rights movement's most recognizable face and leader, King endured constant and overwhelming stress. Stress-related predicaments lead to distractions and inhibit our sense of normalcy. In the case of the distressed King, his crisis led to distractions from his family life, his pastoral duties, and his overwhelming responsibilities with the movement. King's leadership role then brought about unavoidable and uncomfortable life events.

After a particularly strenuous day, a weary King responded to a late-evening telephone call. Through this transmission with an antagonist, he heard a voice filled with opprobrium. That was not unusual either; however, this time it was different. King discerned that the caller was representative of something ominous and even demonic. King took seriously what the caller said. His antagonist was determined to destroy him. Continuous spurious death threats forced King to accept his deep suffering and his experience with fear. Often it is fear that activates faith in desperate circumstances.

This episode that King described is commonly referred to as the "kitchen-table experience." In the middle of his existential crisis, the fearful King recognized and understood that he heard an inner voice, which he identified to be that of Divinity. This voice was clear, quiet, assuring, and undeniable. It is Divinity that declares to humanity that we have an advocate and that we are not alone in our crisis. This assurance was the root of King's testimony, which points toward this chapter's point of departure: we need to have some kind of personal experience and witness to affirm that we have had an authentic encounter with Divinity.

The Limitations of Language about Divinity

Without the voice and presence of Divinity, it is difficult to testify that Divinity is a transcendent and personal Deity. Throughout his public life, King claimed that Divinity reveals Divinity's self and can be personally known. In chapter 2 I pointed toward King's detachment from some of neoorthodoxy's principal themes. One claim King refuted was that Divinity is beyond knowing: "In an attempt to preserve the transcendence of God, which had been neglected by liberalism's overstress of his immanence, neo-orthodoxy went to the extreme of stressing a God who was hidden, unknown and 'wholly other.'"[2]

I consider this theological statement to be another sign that a paradigm shift began in King's theology. The shift represents King's past, present, and forthcoming understanding of Divinity. Indeed, Divinity is not beyond knowing; otherwise, King's telling of his encounter is misleading and intellectually dishonest. I, however, contend that Divinity resists human language, that human language at its best can only refer to and defer to Divinity. In other words, language is referential and deferential.

One scholar argues that there is a nexus between referential and deferential language. In addition, we need to acknowledge the possibility that the Black social gospel and Black theology are born in this way. The Black social gospel is grounded in pragmatism, by which I mean pulling two ideas into tension and forcing observers to make ethical choices:

> [W. E. B.] Du Bois drinks fully from both streams [philosophy and Black religious beliefs] from pragmatist and African American tra-

> ditions. . . . Du Bois transforms both the American philosophical tradition and African religious thought. By [pulling different tensions together]—by embracing religious resources to address . . . the realities of race—Du Bois creates a new faith: a radical version of pragmatic religious naturalism that displays a grasp of sociopolitical implications of pragmatist thought that is more powerful than pragmatists themselves. Du Bois inaugurates a line of African American pragmatic religious naturalism.[3]

It is plausible to suggest that Du Bois is an ancestor of the Black social gospel and Black theology (I will address this thoroughly later in this chapter). Here we grasp that such a theology has pragmatic roots that use referential and deferential language to describe the voice and presence of Divinity. Du Bois, however, envisions that Divinity is a liberator and is political—Divinity takes the side of the oppressed against empire, hegemonic practices, and white supremacy. Furthermore, Du Bois uses language prophetically, reaching beyond our current sights, sounds, smells, and zip codes, and hurls his words into the ether. He does not know the outcome of his prophecy but expects Divinity to act. Nevertheless, there is a problem with language. It is inadequate for a full expression and description of Divinity.

Thus, language at its best is only descriptive and approximate. In short, I believe this adds plausibility to my developing argument. Because of the inherent limitations of language, King employed a metaphorical process that informed his theology. This is evidenced by his consistent use of living words or living metaphors. Thus, I posit that living metaphor underlies King's theological worldview. The following statement by scholar Sallie McFague may provide for readers understanding of my view of the polished King's metaphorical process: "If [post]modernity were the only criterion, our task would be relatively easy. But such is never the case in theology. Christian theology is always an interpretation of 'Gospel' in a particular time and place. So the other task of equal importance is to show that a metaphorical theology is indigenous to Christianity, not just in the sense that it is permitted, but is called for. And this I believe is the case."[4]

I agree that Christian theology is an interpretation of the gospel, but some interpretations are more plausible than others. Still, language has inherent limitations whether it is used referentially or deferentially. Language is a human invention that continues to evolve as humanity and its cultures do the same. Language is an expression of different human perceptions. And language is indigenous to differing cultures and cultural constructs. McFague rightly points out that "metaphorical theology is indigenous to Christianity."

The Twilight of Modernity

To this I add that King's use of metaphorical theology, which is a part of his metaphorical process, is a postmodern and poststructural invention. Postmodernity is defined in various ways. One definition is that it is after (post) modernity. I further claim that postmodernity is after Eurocentric archetypes, symbols, and hegemonies. Postmodernity is accepting globalized worldviews, differing cultures and people groups, and differing interpretations and belief systems that exist independently from the white gaze.

> Too many theories of postmodernity or flexible accumulation speak from within an unquestioned Euro-American perspective that assumes the implosion of time and space to be a process of equally accessible and appreciable, rather than one realized from distinct [multicultural] positions. The academic [white] gaze focused on the condition of postmodernity in the singular, as a systemic process of capital restructuring is a particular and an interested one.[5]

On the one hand, modernity is a European construct with "the basic features of early modern European culture where there was an increasing acceptance of the authority of science, the appearance of a new kind of pagan neoclassicism and the subjectivist turn in philosophy."[6]

On the other hand, this new postmodern paradigm of knowledge considers that hypothetical tests must be used to produce unbiased ends. In theory, all truth claims begin as subjectivist claims. Scientific claims begin as subjective hypotheses that seek absolute objectivism. Furthermore, the truth claims of modernity were accepted to be nearly if not completely absolute. European ideas and culture were considered above contradiction. Thus, cultural and racial biases are inherently grounded in modernity.

The Polished King Conceived a New Theology

Modernity was ghastly toward people of color. What is more, hegemonic systems were built on an intersection between racism and capitalism, resulting in free labor. The following excerpt from Cornel West points to King's rising prominence in the 1950s and to the declining ideological influences of modernity:

> The decline of European modernity between 1871 and 1950—from the unification of the German empire to the emergence of the United States as the unquestioned supreme world power—occurred within the political and socioeconomic contours of an increasingly crisis-ridden monopoly—capitalist world economy. This yielded devastating world wars, holocaust-producing fascist regimes and sharp reaction against repressive Communist governments. The dominated classes in industrial nations—including victims of racist and sexist oppression—flexed their political muscles more in this period and embarked on various courses toward inclusion in and ineffective opposition to the liberal capitalist order.[7]

West paints a bleak portrait and a scathing critique of modernity as a culture. He claims that at its core, modernity has misguided materialistic priorities. These priorities have had devastating effects on what it means to be human. Materialism, which is modernity's god, is the root of materialistic regimes (1 Timothy 6:10). European domination, which is modernity, possessed hegemonic economic power over world markets. Hedonistic materialism was and is accomplished by unification of empires that continue to cause worldwide wars. Materialism gone awry can be pointed to as a singular cause for entrenched class struggles and strife-ridden race and gender clashes. In this context, King came to leadership in the fullness of time (Galatians 4:4).

In 1932 W. E. B. Du Bois provoked conversations around the rising influence of capitalistic regimes and contrasted their influence with the commitments made by Mohandas Gandhi. Du Bois approved of Gandhi's methodology because, he claimed, "What we need in America . . . [is] a Gandhi who will fight the cause of the oppressed. One who, like Gandhi, can divorce himself from the greed of gold, one who can appreciate the misery of the oppressed and respond in spirit to their needs and requirements."[8] What Du Bois described is the emerging polished King. Perhaps providentially, King came into prominence during the twilight of modernity. His appearance signed modernity's death certificate.

In fact, King's postmodern theology eulogizes the death of modernity. In so many words, King's theology is a part of representation I described earlier as advent and what I will soon describe as the birth of postmodernity and poststructuralism. King's postmodernity is compatible with his theological socio-human justice motifs and homiletic commitments. Later I will add to King's theology what is characterized as his Pentecost experience. All of these are underscored by King's appropriation of living metaphor, which supports the polished King's metaphorical process.

As indicated, King's theology grew from his existential crisis and is a response to and resistance against hegemonic, sociopolitical, and socioeconomic conditions imposed on him and other socio-marginalized people. Furthermore, King's response was organized by his adept employment of rhetoric, which supported his theological form, which he used to craft chronicles of the human conditions of his day—conditions caused by unrelenting hegemonic practices that manifested as white supremacy and other forms of oppression.

The polished King's theology was like a mirror that was directed toward his antagonists. In their reflection they could see bereft vanguards of a bereft modernity's status quo. King's mirror also made visible their refusal to acknowledge collective resistance against the changing times that occurred in the 1950s and '60s in America. I believe the civil rights era caused the death of modernity. During that same period, Miles Davis recorded a jazz magnum opus. The recording resisted modern musical structures, which led to more free-flowing styles, melodies, and rhythms. Davis called his record the *Birth of the Cool.* It parallels King's theology and activism and represents the birth of cool, which is postmodernity.

Strands of the Grapevine

Therefore, we take on the task of grasping King's postmodern, poststructuralist theology. At the outset, I claim that to comprehend the polished

King, we must take note of how he used living words. Living metaphor serves as a connector between King's hermeneutic, narrative, rhetoric, and theology, and later his ethical homiletic (see chapter 5). These different disciplines intersect and form King's metaphorical process. Each part can be considered as a separate discipline, but I believe these are nearly inseparable. King's metaphorical process is somewhat like a tightly intertwined grapevine. The life of the vine is dependent on all the intertwining strands. Without one of these strands, the vine could be prevented from natural reproduction. Without reproduction, the grapevine is no longer useful to support the vine grower's family economically (see Matthew 7:18-20). King's theology is part of an interdependent and interdisciplinary system. This is the metaphorical process, but there is more.

King's emergent theology, for example, is not only interdependent and interdisciplinary but also demonstrates that all species of theology at some point intertwine with personal witnesses and testimonies. King's theology emerged and was conceived during his experiences and existential crisis between 1955 and 1968. This is an oversimplification, however. What is not an oversimplification is that King's theology symbolizes a paradigm shift toward a new theology. I define theology this way: *Divinity is revelation capable and willing of self-disclosure to humanity*. Theology, then, is a shared phenomenon between Divinity and humanity. Divinity encodes and humanity decodes the message. We see this in the incarnation of Jesus of Nazareth (John 1:14).

Again, I posit that King's emergent theology began as a response to his undeniable visitation from Divinity, his experience of Divinity as revelation. Divinity transverses and transcends space and comes alongside us in solidarity during both times of peace and times of existential crisis. Divinity's voice, presence, and solidarity underscore that we are creatures to be respected, and that we are destined to live with equality, dignity, and fellowship with all other human bodies and souls. Like King, we are advocates for human equality, and we, too, are in solidarity with oppressed people and share our common pursuit of socio-human and socioeconomic justice. We are assigned and charged with identifying and making visible hegemonic webs spun to entangle us (2 Corinthians 4:4).

Personalism and the Black Social Gospel

What I have described above is close to personalism. This is a species of theology King was formally exposed to throughout his academic career. It began while he was an apprentice within the Black church culture. Prior to attending Boston University, King, according to scholar Gary Dorrien, was formally taught personalism while attending Morehouse College. Benjamin May, Walter Chivers, and George Kelsey exposed King to this liberal theological discipline. During his seminary years, King began to grasp the intersection between Morehouse College's personalism and Kantian and socialist versions. Whatever variation of the theological personalism, it fit Black church culture and preaching philosophically and this Led to King attending Boston University.[9]

Dorrien makes a salient point: King was exposed to forms of personalism that were recognizable and compatible with, though not exactly like, his Black church and cultural experience. What is more, personalism, like Black liberation theology, focuses on the inherent dignity and equality of all persons regardless of their orientations or abilities (or lack thereof). King's theology then has a historical antecedent.

King's antecedent is the Black social gospel. The Black social gospel informed and influenced the civil rights movement. Disappointingly, many scholars remain unaware that there is a Black social gospel, which earlier I associated with the pragmatist W. E. B. Du Bois. In his writings, Du Bois used language referentially and deferentially to employ pragmatic philosophical leanings that intersect with and inform African American religious traditions. Thus, Du Boisian prophetic tradition is an ancestor of the Black social gospel, Black liberation theology, and ensuing protest movements in the 1920s and '30s and in the 1950s and '60s.[10]

The Black social gospel has left an indelible imprint on the American socioreligious landscape. Early Black social gospel leaders were not all clergy. These leaders neither included nor attached biblical and theological doctrines or motifs to their liberation motifs. In short, like Du Boisian pragmatism, Black social gospel is a philosophical and theological construct:

> Black social gospel leaders of the 1920s and 1930s had to negotiate harsh criticism of the Black church by leading experts on this sub-

> ject, especially Du Bois and historians Carter G. Woodson, E. Franklin Frazier, and Rayford Logan. Du Bois and Woodson had lovers' quarrels with the Black church, while Frazier and Logan were more deeply averse to religion per se, but in both cases social gospel leaders countered that Christian faith, critical rationality, and civil rights advocacy went together or at least needed to do so, exactly as Du Bois and Woodson said they should. [Mordecai] Johnson, [Benjamin] Mays, [Howard] Thurman, and others drew on their training in white universities and seminaries to make this argument, inevitably raising the question of whether white academic criticism of any kind belonged in the Black church.[11]

Thus, there are similarities between Black social gospel, Black philosophy, and Black theology. These intersections between secular and sacred representations have one objective: liberation from hegemonic oppressors. During the birth of the Black social gospel, and like the civil rights eras of the 1950s and '60s, there were persons who did not attach a religious narrative to their liberation motifs. Like Johnson, Mays, and Thurman, King understood this intersection, and I suggest this had influence on King's maturing theology and application. Still, Black social gospel tries to resist the white gaze of the white social gospel.

Differences between Black and White Social Gospels

Therefore, the Black social gospel differs from the white social gospel. This is an important differentiation to make because it adds to our understanding of King's emergent theology:

> The founders of the Black social gospel had key affinities with their sometime allies in the white social gospel and Progressive movements. They conceived the federal government as an indispensable guarantor of constitutional rights and principles of justice; they espoused typical Progressive beliefs about equality, politics, and social progress; and they wrestled with modern challenges to religious belief. But Black social gospel leaders addressed these things differently from white progressives, for racial oppression trumped everything

> in the African American context and refigured how other problems were experienced.[12]

As mentioned, noticeable differences exist between Black and white social gospels. The white social gospel is underlined by Kantian philosophy, which represents a paradigm shift that defines an ideological movement from claims of objective propositions that Kantian philosophy believes are flawed. Immanuel Kant sought to establish more exacting objective claims. His thought caused a riptide of debates about the nature of truth. Proponents of Kantian philosophy argue that scientific claims are valued above other claims, including religious propositions. Philosophers before and like Kant believed that religious claims are not infallible. Thus, proponents of Kantian thought further argued that we have perceptions only of truth and reality.

Although it is in search of objectivist claims, Kantian philosophy is subjectivist and grounded in cultural biases. For example, Kantian thought elevates Eurocentric archetypes and ideas about morality above all other possible perceptions and claims. These are clearly examples of hegemonic practices, or what is more commonly known as white supremacy. Said another way, Kantian thought is racist and gender-biased. I emphatically point out that white supremacy is patriarchal and matriarchal.[13]

There is no doubt that Enlightenment philosophers supported white supremacy. Such views were reinforced by thinkers like David Hume, whose view about racial superiority points directly toward Eurocentric proslavery arguments that unjustly denied Black suffrage. A primary example of such denial was ashen anti-Black education propaganda.[14] Hume deeply influenced Kant and the later development of his philosophical construct. Kant's philosophy then led to intellectually sophisticated but morally bankrupt supremacist and hegemonic racial views. Kant wrote, "The [N]egroes of Africa have by nature no feeling that rises above trifling."[15]

Because Kantian thought informs the white social gospel philosophically and theologically, it caused reasonable suspicion from proponents of the Black social gospel. As a result, most Black folks continue to promote deep suspicion and thorough critique of anatomists' objections and resistance to matters of Black lives. Eurocentric theology, another expression of modernity, is philosophically informed and grounded in Eurocentric archetypes and hegemonic cultural claims. The aspirations for equality of those who live in Black bodies and do not thoroughly critique Eurocentric theological claims are hindered. The immediate inclusion of Black bodies into the human family may not be a priority for white social gospel proponents. There are reasons to believe that white social gospel theology is informed by racist constructs.

Another difference between Black and white social gospels and theologies is the interpretation of Christological suffering.[16] The epitome of human suffering is the Jesus event on the cross. From the theological perspective of the Black social gospel, white social gospel proponents lack a serious critique of the suffering of Black bodies, as the prophetic King writes:

> I see a young girl. She is sitting on the stoop of a rickety wooden one-family house in Birmingham. Some visitors would call it a shack. It needs paint badly and the patched-up roof appears in danger of caving in. . . . She can no longer attend the all-Negro school in her neighborhood because her mother died only recently after a car accident. . . . The girl's father is a porter in a downtown department store. He will always be a porter, for there are no promotions for a Negro in a store, where every counter serves him except the one that sells hot dogs and orange juice.[17]

King's theological concerns are embedded in this narrative. Now let us compare King's narrative with Eurocentric postmodern theological concerns. By placing his main character on a stoop outside her family's home, King created geographical boundaries that set his readers' expectations. The home is described like those common to oppressed people in the 1950s and '60s Black American South. King focused on the girl's ambition, which is to learn.

King's womanist character is representative of all children who possess both natural and instinctive intellectual curiosity in all of its various forms—regardless of body, race, gender, or other orientations.[18] As a Black male, the father had no hope of self-improvement. His intellectual curiosities and expectations had long been denied and destroyed because of the South's racial and gender castes and income and wealth gaps, also known as the value gap.[19] Socio-racism functioned as an unbridled and unrivaled anachronistic culture of violence and death in Birmingham, Alabama, in the 1950s and '60s.

King demonstrated that white America doesn't show much concern for the suffering of those who are not white. Their pain does not garner empathy, which is a moral response that points directly to the failure of the white social gospel and its successors. (We can point to the tone-deaf and spiritual numbness of Eurocentric evangelical theology and culture as well.) Eurocentric postmodern theology has an inability to address the suffering of Jesus of Nazareth, the Jesus event on the cross, and Black suffering. Empathy for the suffering Black body in both instances is absent.

The absence of a thorough and robust critique of human suffering is avoidance of the reality that the culture of violence and death causes irreparable human pain. This absence provided indispensable rhetorical space for King's social Black gospel and postmodern theology. King's theology and the Black social gospel are other ways to critique the motivations of the proponents of the white social gospel. What remains in question is their universal liberation commitments, which currently include reparations claims. In addition, I place under critique their understanding of the obvious parallel that exists between the Jesus event on the cross and the human suffering of Black bodies.[20]

I see this as a trope of signification.[21] For example, proponents of the Black social gospel are deeply concerned about the spectacle of lynching Black bodies for no other reason than to prevent erotic and sadistic pleasures for the psychologically disturbed. Unlimited factual evidence exists that white liberal Christians and theologians have not recognized the obvious symbolism between Jesus' crucifixion and the lynchings of Black bodies:

> That the analogy between the cross and the lynching tree should have eluded the Christian agents of white supremacy is perhaps not surprising. But how do we understand the failure of even the most "progressive" of America's white theologians and religious thinkers to make this connection? A case in point is Reinhold Niebuhr, widely regarded as America's most influential theologian in the twentieth century, and possibly in American history. Among his contemporaries he was unusually attuned to social reality and the "irony" and tragedy of American history. Among white theologians he was particularly sensitive to the evils of racism and spoke and wrote on many occasions of the sufferings of African Americans.

> Few theologians of the twentieth century focused as much attention on the cross, one of the central themes of his work. To reflect on this failure is to address a defect in the consciousness of white Christians and to suggest why African Americans have needed to trust and cultivate their own theological imagination.[22]

James Cone's insights parallel King's theological and sociopolitical worldview, which informs and is informed by his protest movement. What is more, King's worldview indicates his departure from theological claims of the white social gospel. Here King differed with Eurocentric modern theology. Since the English settlement at Jamestown, Black folks were not and are not considered equally human. Therefore, some whites still rationalize that Blacks and others are not eligible for universal human rights and suffrage.[23]

Thus, and in addition, for no other reason than economic rights, some whites are antagonists who cannot conceive of Black equality under any circumstances. This is not meant to be hyperbolic; we need only witness the horrendous episodes of contemporary public Black lynchings. Indeed, Black lives continue not to matter. In response, we are witnesses and chroniclers in real time of a revival of the Black social gospel as protest movements have evolved into a Black hybrid of postmodern theology and have taken on poststructural form. This distances Black folks from the white gaze. Current Black protest movements are parallels to the various species of Black liberation motifs (including Black liberation theological claims).

The Black Social Gospel and Protest Movements

Historically, Black social gospel theology grew from a protest movement. As was true during the King years, the theology of the Black social gospel was revealed in the protest movement of the 1920s and '30s. The Black social gospel movement and emergent Black postmodern theology is represented in King's version. Thus, King's theology is a response that represents a resistance movement against hegemonic practices and imperialism. King was a direct heir to his ancestors' theology and made it his own. He added adaptations that were necessary for him to retell the events of the civil rights movement. I reemphasize that King's theology emerged as a response to the existential crisis caused by resistance to hegemonic practices.

Similarities exist between the original Black social gospel and King's movement and theology. Both were born of protests, and both have informed the mature thinking of the polished King's narrative, rhetoric, and theology. Indeed, King's theology is located in his narrative. What is more, King's rhetoric helps readers locate his theological claims that are hidden in plain sight. Rhetoric arranges King's narrative, and we see his theology rising above his oral and written texts.

Postmodernism, Poststructuralism, and King's Thought

Evidence strongly suggests that postmodernity and poststructuralism were informants for King. Ironically, the polished King likely knew that his theology indirectly influenced his aforementioned informants. Postmodernity and poststructuralism are interdependent and nearly inseparable, which means that postmodernity resists what is commonly known as the Eurocentric dominating grand narrative. Poststructuralism replaces the white subject matter, which is decentering, and creates new subjects by way of creating narratives. "Detranscendentalizing the subject . . . [is] a matter of the decentering of the subject."[24]

Du Bois is our example of a postmodern intellectual and religionist. He also is an example of a poststructuralist writer, in that he decentralized the white subject and replaced it with subjects of his choosing:

> This is the story of a human heart,—the tale of a black boy who many long years ago began to struggle with life that he might know the world and know himself. Three temptations he met on those dark dunes that lay gray and dismal before the wonder-eyes of the child: the temptation of Hate, that stood out against the red dawn; the temptation of Despair, that darkened noonday; and the temptation of Doubt, that ever steals along with twilight. Above all, you must hear of the vales he crossed,—the Valley of Humiliation, and the Valley of the Shadow of Death.25

In this passage, Du Bois decentered white intellectual superiority by offering Alexander Crummell as representative of Black intellectual equality with others, including whites. This is an early poststructural text.

Du Bois knew that the white gaze must be deconstructed or decentered in order to enhance the emergent Black self-affirmation that comes from orators and writers placing their "heroes and sheroes" in the center of their texts as subjects and not as objects. This supports my assertion that King's version of postmodern theology is a postmodern and poststructuralist response to the Eurocentric, anachronistic construct of modernity.

Like proponents of modernity, the proponents of Eurocentric postmodernity are guardians of a status quo. Postmodernity is a hybrid of cultures that reluctantly expands the Western canon of letters to include newer voices, however selective the vanguards continue to be. Postmodernity then can be further defined in at least two ways. First, postmodernity is an antithetical invention and a response against the conventional claims of modernity. Second, postmodernity is a creature of multiculturalism. Jean-François Lyotard, a scholar of philosophy defined postmodernity as follows:

> I define postmodernity as incredulity toward metanarratives. This incredulity is undoubtedly a product of progress in the sciences: but that progress in turn presupposes it. To the obsolescence of the metanarrative apparatus of legitimation corresponds, most notably, the crisis of metaphysical philosophy and of the university institution which in the past relied on it. The narrative function is losing its functors, its great hero, its great dangers, its great voyages, its great goal. It is being dispersed in clouds of narrative language elements—narrative, but also denotative, prescriptive, descriptive, and so on. Conveyed within each cloud are pragmatic valences specific to its kind. Each of us lives at the intersection of many of these. However, we do not necessarily establish stable language combinations, and the properties of the ones we do establish are not necessarily communicable.[26]

And as Terry Eagleton, a scholar of English literature reports, postmodernity ideally is representative of multiculturalism, which envisions that all cultural narratives are of equal value: "What bred the culture of postmodernism, with its dismissal of so-called grand narratives and triumphal announcement of the End of History, was above all the conviction that the future would now be simply more of the present. Or, as one exuberant postmodernist put it, 'The present plus more options.'"[27]

Taking these two scholars' definitions into consideration, postmodern theology has identifiable traits. First, postmodernity resists metanarratives, and second, postmodernity embraces multiculturalism. Both traits inform postmodern theology.

King's theology emerged in the waning hours of the anachronistic culture of modernity. I contend that King was aware that his version of postmodern theology differed from that of Eurocentric postmodernism. By that I mean King's theology resisted new hegemonic claims over interpretation, narrative, rhetoric, theology, homiletics, and ethics. King did not seek cultural approval from the vanguards over Eurocentric postmodern claims in order to proceed with his socio-human, socioeconomic, and sociopolitical demands that action be taken to bring about socio-racism liberation. Instead, King's postmodern theology was a response to his and others' existential crises.

Like most Eurocentric philosophical constructs, postmodernity and its proponents are flawed in large part because of biases against others' worldviews. Left to their own Eurocentric impulses, proponents of postmodernity, like the proponents of modernity, try to control and influence institutional spheres and infrastructures. As Eagleton writes,

> Postmodern apostles of plurality need to be more pluralistic about the notion. They should abandon the formalist dogma that it is always and everywhere to be extolled, whatever its actual content. If they were to do so, they might come to recognize in more pragmatic spirit that difference and diversity are sometimes beneficial and sometimes not. . . . Being more diverse about diversity, as well as acknowledging that difference may differ from one context to the other, would signal a genuine breakthrough for such [postmodernist] thinkers.[28]

Eurocentric biases occur despite claims from proponents of postmodernity; that is, we are against grand narratives and therefore we support multicultural diversity. However, there are many diversity initiatives that have been excluded historically. Not until recently have initiatives such as mass incarceration reform, universal healthcare, and access to tuition-free higher education at public colleges and universities been supported.

In contrast, King's postmodern theology resists all forms of human exclusion. Paradoxically, human inclusion preserves Black folks' lives. King's theology then emerges as representative of the birth of postmodern culture, but his species of postmodern theology is not to be mistaken as an extension or an affirmation of another authoritative or more gravely authoritarian Eurocentric construct. King's theology may share some Eurocentric postmodern existential traits, but his theology remains largely independent of the white gaze to protect human rights from anarchists. King's theology supports those who share his moral imperatives in pursuit of justice. King's theology then primarily remains informed by his predecessors, who are the founders and proponents of the Black social gospel and its corresponding movement.

King's Fight against Nihilism

More narrowly, King's postmodern theology is interdependent with other aspects of his metaphorical process. As a whole, King's theology addresses his fight against nihilism. Hidden underneath racism and other forms of oppression is nihilism. Cornel West, a scholar of philosophy and religion, explains that nihilism is Black people's existential threat that continued after King was martyred. Nihilism surfaces as crisis and is the perpetual threat to the survival of Black America (we now include other socio-marginalized people):

> *Nihilism is to be understood here not as a philosophical doctrine that there are no rational grounds for legitimate standards of authority; it is, far more, the lived experience of coping with a life of horrifying meaninglessness, hopelessness, and (most important) lovelessness.* The frightening result is a numbing detachment from others and a self-destructive disposition toward the world. Life without meaning, hope, and love breeds a coldhearted, mean-spirited outlook that destroys both the individual and others.[29]

West writes as a postmodernist in the Du Boisian prophetic tradition and is concerned with the conditions of Black people in America who face the intrusion of nihilism.[30] Perhaps more bluntly, Black people are at risk of psychological and spiritual detachment from what most others would recognize as reality. What is blunter, this distorted view imposes altered realities upon those who are possessed by it. They accept distortions as normalized reality.

Distorted realities or detachments are a result of imperial power. This is uncovered by taking critical notice of hegemonic practices. As an example, in Mark's gospel, Jesus asked the name of a man who was possessed by many demons. The possessed man cried that his name was "Legion ... for we are many" (Mark 5:9). Legion or Roman legions signify that the Roman occupation in the land of the Gadarenes was at least metaphorically an occupation of demons that harass people and leave many psychologically dysfunctional. These practices are identifiable in our current struggles with hegemonic and imperial forces which are demonic catalysts for racism and economic exploitation. This exploitation thwarts social cohesion of Black families. Limited economic mobility is historic, predictable, and unavoidable evidence that disproportionate unemployment leads to disproportionate breakdowns in our collective fabric that protects our social underpinnings. We recognize such breakdowns as the source of Black folks' deep sense of human emptiness and perilous void of hope in the future. This is nihilism and nothingness.

The intersection between nihilism and nothingness has not been unnoticed or resolved. In fact, theology's goal and task is to locate the presence of Divinity in the midst of oppression and during the oppressed pursuit of being. This can be difficult during revolutionary change as during the civil rights era (1955–68). As a Baptist preacher and public theologian, King understood and explained that socio-human change threatens hegemonic power enjoyed and reinforced by the vanguards of the status quo. Nihilism and nothingness are located in the vanguard's hegemonic systems:

> Not until I entered theological seminary, however, did I begin a serious quest for a method to eliminate social evil. I was immediately influenced by the social gospel. In the early [1950s] I read [Walter] Rauschenbusch's *Christianity and the Social Crisis*, a book which left an indelible imprint on my thinking. Of course there are points at which I differed with Rauschenbusch. . . . But in spite of these

> shortcomings Rauschenbusch gave to America Protestantism a sense of social responsibility that it should never lose. The gospel at its best deals with the whole man [and woman], not only his [or her] soul, but his body, not only his [or her] spiritual being, but his [or her] material well-being. Any religion that professes to be concerned about the souls of men [and women] and is not concerned about the slums that damn them, the economic conditions that strangle them and the social conditions that cripple them is a spiritually moribund religion awaiting burial.[31]

In another speech, King stated:

> To the Negro, as 1963 approached, the economic structure of society appeared to be so ordered that a precise sitting of jobs took place. The lowest-paid employment and the most tentative jobs were reserved for him [or her]. If he [or her] sought to change his [or her] position, he was walled in by the tall barriers of discrimination. As summer came, more than ever the spread of unemployment had visible and tangible dimensions to the colored American. Equality meant dignity and dignity demanded a job that was secure and a paycheck that lasted throughout the week.[32]

King stood against humanly engineered systems developed to manipulate, exploit, and suppress people's socio-human upward mobility. His philosophical, theological, and economic motifs define his moral imperatives. We locate these in his version of the Black social gospel.

It is further noteworthy that King's social gospel imperatives differ from those of Walter Rauschenbusch. Rauschenbusch's understanding of the kingdom of God, for example, King explained, is attached to a "particular economic system." King disagreed. He discounted all sociopolitical and socioeconomic systems that he believed were corrupted, and neither did he accept that oppressed people can wait for transformed human motivations to acknowledge that oppressed people are equally human. King alleged that Rauschenbusch did not detach himself from white privilege, which we know capitalism underscores. This economic system, without radical decentering, deconstruction, and transformation, causes collateral and direct damage to oppressed people.[33]

In comparison with Rauschenbusch's worldview, the polished King understood that the kingdom of God or the universal church cannot be authentic unless it stands against oppressive worldly social, economic, and political systems. King expected the church to be responsible for uplifting the whole person. King's position was similar to the parable in which Jesus of Nazareth explained the importance of separating the wheat from the tares. The authentic church is recognized in harvest season (Matthew 13:24-30). This is located at the root of King's ecclesial theology. Aspects of King's personalist theology are located in human worth and dignity.

King's exposure to personalism may be adaptable to his understanding of the Black social gospel. Both are concerned with the whole person. In other words, King's theology is concerned with taking a stand against all demonic systems that reinforce human deficits. This highlights that King's major influence was the Black social gospel, which I believe is the primary reason he denounced any religion unconcerned with dismantling all sociohuman and socioeconomic constructs that entangle humanity in demonic hegemonic webs of oppression. This is an explanation for King's departure from the white social gospel and the theology, capitalism, and white privilege of Rauschenbusch.

What is certain, the liberating King was disquieted and agitated by the human conditions of Black people. King as a public theologian and leader of the civil rights movement understood that he confronted multidimensional and complex opponents. Among these were white supremacy and Black low self-esteem. However, King's larger opponent, which was nihilism and nothingness, lurked beneath the surface. Not until now have I defined nihilism and nothingness as symptoms of fear. To liberate Black and white people from fear, we, like King, must confront what causes fear. We see causes such as racism, economic privilege, manipulation of politics, and dysfunctional psychological and theological underpinnings. These are nearly inseparable strands of the same grapevine, in other words, interdependent.

King understood that these nearly inseparable strands had an intertwining role in his liberation process. Otherwise, achieving human justice may be impossible:

> Racial segregation is buttressed by such irrational fears as loss of preferred economic privilege, altered social status, intermarriage, and adjustment to new situations. Through sleepless nights and haggard days, numerous white people attempt to combat these corroding fears by diverse methods. By following the path of escape, some seek to ignore the question of race relations and to close their mind to the issues involved. Others, placing their faith in such legal maneuvers as interposition and nullification, counsel massive resistance. . . . But how futile are all these remedies! Instead of eliminating fear, they instill deeper and more pathological fears that leave the victims inflicted with strange psychoses and peculiar cases of paranoia. Neither repression, massive resistance, nor aggressive violence will cast out the fear of integration; only love and goodwill can do that.[34]

In the preceding passages, we notice that fear emerges as an emotional response to whites losing their preferred economic privilege and social status. This is a construct of economics and racism. Their fear of intermarriage is also a construct of racism and economic privilege. King highlighted sleeplessness experienced by fearful whites by pointing out that they spent precious rest time devising divisive laws, which are a construct of racism and politics. In the second passage, King focused on pathology and paranoia, repression, resistance, and violence instead of love. These are constructs of racism and psychology. Only love and good as liberatory actions to be taken are constructs of King's theology.

These are useful examples that lead to grasping King's sense of dangerous presence and the effects of nihilism and nothingness. Fear and emptiness drive humanity toward irrational behaviors. Furthermore, these examples provide insight into King's cultural worldview. His theology uncovers and reinforces his strategic campaign to demand socio-human and socioeconomic justice. Economic justice for many is a declaration of cultural war. America's political right understands clearly that there is an intersection between race, politics, economics, and white privilege.[35] For example, Pat Buchanan said an adversarial and libertine culture was jeopardizing the very integrity of the republic. "As America's imperial troops guard frontiers all over the world," he said, "our own frontiers are open, and the barbarian is inside the gates.

And you do not deal with Vandals and Visigoths who are pillaging your cities by expanding the Head Start and food stamps programs."[36]

Buchanan spoke as the canary in the coal mine. He sounded the alarm that the mine's scaffolding was collapsing. Some would be injured, and others would die, but the scaffolding must be repaired, maintained, inspected, and guarded. Otherwise, economic privilege and homogenous survival would be compromised and possibly lost forever. Those who heard him doubled down, and decades later continue to support state-sponsored policies that hinder the upward economic mobility and family stability of Blacks and other marginalized people.

Those who support economic depravity, exploitation, and hegemonic practices are treasonous to the proposition of democracy. If treasonous, they are confederating, and their fight, then, is misleading and misplaced. What they are fighting is not oppressed people but the fear of emptiness. Their battle is against nihilism and nothingness. Abolishing racism and all forms of hatred leaves us to face the real enemy, which is the self. It is human emptiness that leads to hatred of others. We know this clearly. American racist culture is underpinned by Eurocentric culture. Both reinforce white supremacy.

It is significant also that white supremacy points toward faithful proponents of anachronistic modernity. Still, white supremacy is worthy of protection, some believe. Proponents believe that modernity is not to be disturbed. To do so is to disturb their self-consciousness. Proponents of modernity will not admit to themselves that their cultural underpinnings are flawed with white mythologies, and oftentimes they will not admit guilt or that they are capable of shameful acts toward other human beings.

Proponents of modernity instead enjoy and want to become like their mythological characters. Emotionally, they want to continue (and quite successfully do) producing and writing movies in which their characters are mythological figures that are placed at the center of their narratives. This is deliberate deception. Stubborn faith in modernity reinforces their mythical beliefs in their fictitious sense of racial superiority. Without these mythologies and deceptions, white supremacy is to die a painful death. That death is feared. It means facing nihilism and nothingness.

Like King, who understood this fear, I conclude that proponents of modernity are afraid of acknowledging their perception of the arriving shadows of nihilism and nothingness. Fear of emptiness is not only among Black Americans but also is deeply rooted in the mainstream of white America's Eurocentric worldview and among the most elite and the most common of white Americans. I point toward the work of Jean-Paul Sartre, a French existentialist whose literary canon is controversial and consequential on the subject of existential fear. He described human fear of the future, human anxieties, and the horror of motives:

> I am the self which I will be, in the mode of not being it. It is through my horror that I am carried toward the future, and the horror nihilates itself in that it constitutes the future as possible. Anguish is precisely my consciousness of being my own future, in the mode of not-being. To be exact, the nihilation of horror as a motive, which has the effect of reinforcing horror as a state, has as its positive counterpart the appearance of other forms of conduct (in particular that which consists in throwing myself over the precipice) *as my possible possibilities*. If *nothing* compels [the italics are Sartre's] me to save my life, *nothing* prevents me from precipitating myself into the abyss.[37]

This excerpt epitomizes my characterization of nihilism and nothingness. The anxious existentialist senses clear and present danger to white psychological well-being. Perhaps it is better described as paranoia. I suggest this is how King understood the threat of nihilism and nothingness. Postmodernity, which I believe manifested in earnest during King's era, is compatible with pluralism (multiculturalism). This may be a way out of nihilism and nothingness.

If postmodernity is representative of pluralism, the grand narrative, then, is to be deconstructed and dismantled. If this happens, it represents post-structuralism (the structure of after-modernity). When the lie is threatened, its proponents feel a sense of rage over being left behind politically, religiously, and economically. Then judgment comes, they feel, for their racist worldview that has led to unnecessary human carnage.

Thus far I have tried to describe the context from which King's theology grew. As the leader of a resistance movement, King faced the most powerful empire the world has ever witnessed. America is an amalgamation of all the world's previous empires (Revelation 13:1-2). This shapes the contours of the leadership King used to confront the American empire. He knows that empire is protected by deference to the grand narrative. That is, empire is an expression of the Eurocentric construct. The construct or constructs are of race, politics, economics, gender, other human differences, and white privilege, mythologies, hegemonies, and supremacies.

Hidden beneath media and literary propaganda schemes are these constructs. In this case, schemes are crafted to retain control. Control or hegemonic practices need the cover of distortions and distractions to maintain socio-human and political divisions. Through these means, the status quo remains deeply entrenched. Underneath the status quo, however, are these deadly sins I have characterized as fear of nihilism and nothingness. In response the proponents of white theology (I am thinking of Rauschenbusch) have not addressed, will not address, or cannot address these deadly sins. I suggest that is because proponents of white theology are a part of empire and support Eurocentric constructs. Whatever the case, these constructs continue to entangle us in sophisticated webs of oppression.

The Experience of Pentecost

Another feature of King's theology I characterize as his Pentecost experience. As this chapter began, the unnerved and threatened King heard the voice and felt the presence of Divinity. This is Pentecost, and we have located the final strand of his theology.

A respected New Testament scholar, F. F. Bruce, commented,

> In the events of the first Christian Pentecost, according to Acts 2, God, who once spoke at Sinai, now spoke again to the nations and confirmed his covenant to pour out his Spirit on all flesh. The putting of God's Spirit within man [and woman] was a sign of the new covenant, as comparison of Jeremiah 31:31ff with Ezekiel 11:19f and 36:25ff makes plain; in view of Jesus' promise it was also a token that he had now been enthroned by God as Lord and Messiah, the effective Baptizer with the Spirit. The call therefore came

> to the whole house of Israel to repent, to accept baptism in the name of Jesus, and thus receive not only the forgiveness of their sins but also the gift of the Spirit.[38]

Bruce locates a chain stitch. That is, the Old Testament prophetic passages point toward a more evolving and mature culture that would recognize that Jesus of Nazareth is Lord and Messiah, the "effective Baptizer with the Spirit." The day of Pentecost, which continues through the entire book of Acts, demonstrates that a theological paradigm shift has occurred and, I suggest, continues to occur.

In Acts the role of the Holy Spirit is part of the emphasis on God's providence. It is primarily through God's Spirit that the community was aware of the divine power at work among them. So central was the work of the Spirit in Acts that some have suggested that a more appropriate title for the book would be the Acts of the Holy Spirit, though the Spirit is not even mentioned in eleven chapters of Acts. Luke gave enough clues in the earlier chapters of Acts for readers to realize that references to the Christians speaking "boldly" and the like indicate that the Spirit was with them. Such indications occur to the last verses of Acts.[39]

Too often we have heard King and the civil rights movement associated with *Zeitgeist*. However, though many mention *Zeitgeist* in reference to King, I believe the day of Pentecost is a better description of his theological worldview. It is Pentecost that he experienced, understood, and embraced. King was empowered by the Spirit to lead the Pentecost movement, the civil rights movement in the 1950s and '60s.

I ground my claim in King's kitchen-table experience. Thus, King's Pentecost experience served as the contour and shape of his theology. I see a parallel between King's and Luke's use of living metaphor. I point to the Acts of the Holy Spirit. Luke's work is divided into twenty-eight chapters. As his story unfolds, there is an emergent chain stitch throughout the work. This chain stitch expresses what I characterize as the manifestation of Divinity, which shapes all languages and cultures. For example, the gospel emerges in Jerusalem. I call this the Jerusalem gospel (Acts 1–8). Next, the gospel spreads to the region of Judea, and therefore I call this the Judean gospel (Acts 8–10). The gospel continues to spread into Samaria, or what I refer to as the Samaritan gospel (Acts 10–13). What follows then is the manifestation of the European gospel (Acts 13–28).

Thus, the Spirit of Pentecost continued, and people heard the gospel in their own languages. Through their own languages, they came to know the voice and presence of Divinity. Throughout Luke's writing, we meet witnesses and hear testimonies about Divinity's opposition to empire. The opposition, according to Luke, began with Spirit-filled languages. Although I have made clear that language is limited and cannot be written or spoken in such a way that it adequately expresses the person of Divinity, I know, too, that language is used for that very purpose. Divinity's spiritual presence is manifest in human language.

According to Luke, the manifestation of the Spirit of Pentecost empowered Galileans to speak in other tongues (Acts 2:4). This phenomenon was not a prayer language (1 Corinthians 14:6-19). Instead, other tongues (*glossa*) are known to be native languages that were spoken by people who were natives of surrounding towns and specific regions. Those who came to Jerusalem to attend the Festival of Harvest heard Galileans speak to them in their own native tongues. These citizens were residents of two competing and dominating empires, the Roman and Parthian Empires (Acts 2:7, 9-11). Language, then, is an expressive act; the Spirit of Pentecost is manifested in multiple languages and therefore cannot be homogenized and limited to hegemonic practices. Instead, the Word of Divinity belongs to multiple people of multiple cultures.

This is a way to acknowledge and confront nihilism and nothingness. That is, the voice and presence of Divinity are recognized in multiple names, faces, and places. In short, Divinity cannot be subjugated or objectified by a dominating people's language and culture. To the contrary, Divinity's voice and active presence usurp and decenter dominating people and their cultural hegemonies. This, however, does not mean that proponents of white supremacy accept this premise. There is cultural, academic, and political resistance: "The study of humanities [which includes theology] is the study of the possibilities of human life in culture. It thrives on diversity," writes Henry Louis Gates Jr.[40] He continues, "The most influential and innovative programs in comparative literature [this includes all disciplines in theological studies] have embraced just three languages—Latin, French, German—and one other [English]. I look forward to truly comparative programs . . . that embrace the languages and literatures of Yoruba, Urdu, or Arabic as well as the traditional European literatures."[41]

Listen to the great author Herman Melville, writing a century earlier:

> There is something in the contemplation of the mode in which America has been settled, that, in a noble breast, should forever extinguish the prejudices of national dislikes. Settled by the people of all nations, all nations may claim her for their own. You cannot spill a drop of American blood, without spilling blood of the whole world. . . . We are not a narrow tribe, no: our blood is as the flood of the Amazon, made up of a thousand noble currents, all pouring into one. We are not a nation, so much as a world.[42]

The requirements of multicultural programs and curriculum are controlled by proponents and vanguards of Eurocentrism. Advanced degrees conferred by most elite American institutions of higher education, for example, require applicants to have had prerequisites or to study European languages during their programs (Latin, French, German, English, and Spanish too). This is cultural hegemony, reinforcing support and policies of Eurocentrism. There are other languages, such as Yoruba, Urdu, and the like. And Melville, part of the nineteenth-century Gilded Age, recognized that proponents of American democracy must be proponents of democracy, which is for all people, all the time, regardless of otherness.

Democracy then faces the ugliness of nihilism and nothingness. And it appears that democracy was the foundation of Luke's day of Pentecost: the Spirit of Pentecost arrived as symbol: "When the day of Pentecost arrived, they were all together in one place. And suddenly there came from heaven a sound like a mighty rushing wind, and it filled the entire house where they were sitting. And divided tongues as of fire appeared to them and rested on each one of them. And they were all filled with the Holy Spirit and began to speak in other tongues as the Spirit gave them utterance" (Acts 2:1-4, ESV).

The Spirit of Pentecost is indeed a symbol but also is representative of democracy. Democracy, then, is representative of multiple languages, multiple cultures, and multiple people, because the Spirit of Pentecost rested upon multiple languages, cultures, and people. Earlier I mentioned that the Spirit spreads across boundaries and moves across competing empires. There is more. As we try to understand symbolism as signification, we must take into careful consideration Luke's adept use of living metaphor. (To signify is to transport meaning by metaphor to another destination.)

Symbolism in the passage from Acts is signification. For example, we must interpret what "a sound like a rushing wind" means. This is a living metaphor, and therefore we know that it links ideas between two spaces. This may be necessary to usurp or decenter a particular dominating culture's psychological self, which is often the only permissible subject (the white male and increasingly the white female).

I have written elsewhere that signification defers meaning and that it may remain dormant until particular cultures evolve. What I refer to as dormant meaning, Gates describes as intermediate meaning:

> The text, in other words, is not fixed in any determinate sense; in one sense, it consists of the dynamic and intermediate relationship between truth on the one hand and understanding on the other. Species of Black preaching use tropes and metaphors to communicate nuanced, if not deferred, meaning; this is consistent with my claim that a rhetorical act can be an example of dormant meaning. For example, I associate my use of dormant meaning with [Chaim] Perelman's comments about dormant metaphor, "This strength is due to the fact that it obtains its effect by drawing on a stock of analogical material that gains ready acceptance because it is not merely known, but it is integrated by language into the cultural tradition." What Perelman describes, functions in rhetoric [which we have argued intertwines with theology among other disciplines] that originate in marginalized subcultures.[43]

King eloquently proclaimed that the era of the dormant is awakened by the voice and presence of Divinity. At the Lincoln Memorial, he stood before multiple peoples and cultures that had evolved and matured to grasp his living metaphor, which is symbolism:

> We have also come to this hallowed spot to remind America of the fierce urgency of now. This is no time to engage in the luxury of cooling off or to take the tranquilizing drug of gradualism. Now is the time to make real the promises of democracy; now is the time to rise from the dark and desolate valley of segregation to the sunlit path of racial justice; now is the time to lift our nation from the quicksands of racial injustice to the solid rock of brotherhood; now is the time to make justice a reality for all God's children. It would be fatal for the nation to overlook the urgency of the moment. This sweltering summer of the Negro's legitimate discontent will not pass until there is an invigorating autumn of freedom and equality.[44]

King used rhetoric to arrange his postmodern theology in this Pentecost moment, which was to "make real the promises of democracy." Postmodernity and poststructuralism are the seedbed for democracy and democratic values, and what is more, democracy cannot occur without multiple faces that represent many languages and cultures, hopes and dreams. Democracy's hope confronts nihilism's nothingness. What King saw is people aligned like a phalanx on each side of the reflecting pool. He shared and uncovered his theology by deploying a repetitious volley of living metaphors. He framed the occasion as the "fierce urgency of now" in contrast to "the tranquilizing drug of gradualism." King used the living metaphor "now is the time" four times in this paragraph. This signifies and emphasizes that the dormant metaphor represents intermediate understanding of justice that is awakened because the time has now come to fulfillment. Take notice of the contrast between "quicksands of racial injustice" and "the solid rock of brotherhood." This is Pentecost rhetoric and theology, or as I have emphasized, this is postmodern and poststructural rhetoric and theology.

Whether we are focused on Luke's or King's narrative and theology, we see their brilliant use of dormant metaphor, which doubles as living metaphor. Further, we see that transported meaning may be disguised as dormant metaphor. That which is dormant is not necessarily dead but can be alive. Signification, as I describe, points to an intermediate meaning. Furthermore, dormant metaphor and living metaphor unloose fixed meaning.

Biblical texts or models, then, are not fixed but in fact are dynamic. Living texts seem to adjust themselves to reach toward people and cultures as we evolve and mature and our understanding increases. We understand Divinity because of revelation, or illumination. Divinity moves toward us. This is the efficacy and sufficiency of Scripture, and to a lesser extent the same can be asserted about our evolving and maturing understanding of the theological King. We are reminded that King's theology emerges in large part because of and through an existential crisis. The crisis is nothing less than trauma.

Like the crucifixion and resurrection of Jesus of Nazareth, the ascension must have caused his followers to feel trauma deeply. In this chapter I characterize trauma as existential crisis. Still, the mysterious nature of Jesus isn't fully understood. Added to the disciples' trauma is the mysterious day of Pentecost. No human language adequately defines this phenomenon. In short, the day of Pentecost is a kind of second incarnation of Divinity (some call this an impartation). This time incarnation is the person of the Holy Spirit, which leads to the Spirit's third incarnation, Divinity's indwelling of the human body, mind, and soul. This indwelling of Divinity has been simultaneously in multiracial bodies and multicultural people groups across the world throughout the ages (John 14:12-17).

Before King's kitchen-table experience, Luke used living metaphor as word symbols that approximated this phenomenon; he recognized the phenomenon as the voice and presence of the Spirit. He expressed the visitation as "a sound like a mighty rushing wind." He conceded that the visitation was not a literal mighty rushing wind, but he does not have adequate words in his lexicon to be exact. His point was that the Spirit came with a loud sound like a powerful wind. He further expressed the Spirit's visitation as "divided tongues as a fire [that] appeared to them and rested on each one of them." Luke described the Spirit's presence, audibility, and visibility as the Spirit appeared as fire and quite possibly generated something like heat that can only be associated with fire. Fire needs oxygen to continue to burn, consume, transform, and refine (Zechariah 13:9; Malachi 3:3; Matthew 3:11).

These are examples of effective use of living metaphor. It is significant that the original witnesses in the Acts of the Holy Spirit bear testimony that they were aware of the mysteriousness of Divinity. In Acts 2:4 is included literal language: "they . . . began to speak in other tongues as the Spirit gave them utterance." The Spirit of Divinity comes in undeniable power. People of multiple cultures and languages have access to Divinity that governments could not prevent. And what is equally significant is that those empowered understood that they had been liberated from nihilism and nothingness, and the evidence of such liberation was their resistance against hegemonic practices. The Pentecost people rejected the status quo, the archetypes, conventions, forms, and functions. This, then, was a type of postmodernity and poststructuralism.

Luke's profound use of living metaphor was a forerunner of postmodernism and poststructuralism. No language is adequate to explain the phenomenon of Pentecost except by understanding the writer; the witnesses, the readers, and the hearers were willing to do the difficult and important work of interpretation of their living narrative that was necessary to construct Pentecost theology. "Whatever criticisms one may level against particular models [of theology], it would be small-minded and ungrateful not to praise models as loosening our tongues to express, however inadequately, the inexpressible."[45]

Words alone are inadequate to give testimony to having heard the voice and felt the presence of Divinity. Still, the theological task is to try—and with words to do so. Thus, like Luke and King, we must grapple in solidarity to communicate the Pentecost experience. We can trace postmodernity and poststructuralism to Luke's retelling of the day of Pentecost. And we can locate contemporary Pentecost theology to King in his time.

Although they are inspired, I reinforce that Luke's words are inadequate to describe the indescribable voice and presence of Divinity. But the attempt had to be made. I believe that Luke understood that Pentecost theology can be grasped only by understanding the role of living metaphor. Living metaphor, then, is a species of signification that is necessary to interpret Luke's double meaning. We see similar traits in King's metaphorical process. Without understanding King's living metaphor, we will struggle to interpret King's use of signifying or double meaning. Paul Ricoeur makes this easier to understand: "I directly defined hermeneutics by an object which seemed to be both as broad and as precise as possible, I mean the symbol. As regards the symbol, I defined it in turn by its semantic structure of having double meaning."[46]

In Black America, double meaning is pervasive, and most understand its double meaning:

I never had to have money befo',
And now they want it everywhere I go.[47]

This excerpt is short but provides us with a pregnant living metaphor. The metaphor is an example of signification and a masterful use of double meaning. After the bondmen's and bondwomen's emancipation from slavery, freedom did not provide liberation. The former slaves did not have access to capital or employment. Instead, the living metaphor, through double meaning, uncovers for us the reality of another form of slavery—economic slavery. The excerpt points to human longing for equality and further points toward a collective demand for justice. And further yet, it points toward existential crisis.

In addition, the Pentecost experience located in Luke's and King's narratives points toward an intersection between democracy and justice. Comprehension of these facts helps us to understand how effective living metaphor is used as a link to uncover powerful symbolism. What follows is how the biblical Pentecost narrative continues in King's narrative. They are similar in this way: both narratives inform Pentecost theology. Said another way, Luke and King's Pentecost is meant to underscore that Divinity deputizes and democratizes our collective effort to achieve human justice. Let's look first at Luke's and then at King's:

> And all who believed were together and had all things in common. And they were selling their possessions and belongings and distributing the proceeds to all, as any had need. And day by day, attending the temple together and breaking bread in their homes, they received their food with glad and generous hearts, praising God and having favor with all the people. And the Lord added to their number day by day those who were being saved. (Acts 2:44-47, ESV)

> I am now convinced that the simplest approach will prove to be the most effective—the solution to poverty is to abolish it directly by a now widely discussed measure: the guaranteed income. . . . The problem [abolishing poverty] indicates that our emphasis must

> be two-fold. We must create full employment or we must create incomes. People must be made consumers by one method or the other. Once they are placed in this position, we need to be concerned that the potential of the individual is not wasted. New forms of work that enhance the social good will have to be devised for those for whom traditional jobs are not available.[48]

King's Pentecost theology is postmodern and poststructural. Democracy and justice for all people groups are not possible in a society where the archetypes of anachronistic modernity function. What is more, like Luke's theology, King's continued to evolve and mature as the civil rights struggles raged throughout the 1950s and '60s.

A final note: Luke the writer and King were chroniclers as much as theologians. Both writers organized and arranged their narratives to be heard and read in real time.[49] What is clear, Divinity is revealed in human language. As stated, our language is limited and cannot adequately express the reality that the voice and presence of Divinity are among multiple people and cultures. King, too, experienced Divinity's voice and presence.

At the root of King's theology, I have posited, is a metaphorical process that is tightly intertwined like a grapevine. That is to say, King's hermeneutic, narrative, rhetoric, and theology intersect and therefore are interdependent. In the next and final chapter, I address King's homiletic. I will feature his sermons that are developed from parables. This will paint a portrait of the polished King and his work during the 1950s and '60s.

Throughout his public ministry, King and his family lived through psychological and spiritual nightmares. They had highs and lows, hopes and doubts, dreams and despairs. Coretta Scott King admitted as much in December 1956 at the Holt Street Church in Montgomery, Alabama. King, in response to his wife, confessed that given the choice, he "would have run away had he seen the whirlwind coming."[50] Yet Divinity is in the whirlwind, and "the choice leaves your own hands."[51]

Notes

1. Martin Luther King Jr., *A Testament of Hope: The Essential Writings and Speeches of Martin Luther King Jr.*, ed. James M. Washington (New York: HarperOne, 1986), 509. See also Martin Luther King Jr., *The Strength to Love* (Minneapolis: Fortress, 2010), 116–17.

2. Martin Luther King Jr., "Pilgrimage to Nonviolence," in *A Testament of Hope: The Essential Writings and Speeches of Martin Luther King Jr.*, ed. James M. Washington (New York: HarperOne, 1986), 36.

3. Jonathan S. Kahn, *Divine Discontent: The Religious Imagination of W. E. B. Du Bois* (Oxford: Oxford University Press, 2009), 13.

4. Sallie McFague, *Metaphorical Theology: Models of God in Religious Language* (Philadelphia: Fortress, 1982), 14.

5. Rosemary J. Coombe and Paul Stoller, "X Marks the Spot: Ambiguities of African Trading in the Commerce of the Black Public Square," in *The Black Public Sphere: A Public Culture Book* (Chicago: University of Chicago Press, 1995), 259.

6. Cornel West, *The Cornel West Reader* (New York: Basic Civitas Books, 1999), 55.

7. West, *Cornel West Reader*, 63.

8. W. E. B. Du Bois, quoted in Gary Dorrien, *Breaking White Supremacy: Martin Luther King Jr. and the Black Social Gospel* (New Haven, CT: Yale University Press, 2018), 9.

9. Dorrien, 19.

10. Dorrien, 45.

11. Dorrien, 6.

12. Dorrien, 3.

13. David Blight, *Frederick Douglass: Prophet of Freedom* (New York: Simon and Schuster, 2018). Elizabeth Cady Stanton was bitter toward Frederick Douglass, who courageously supported Black men receiving the right to vote. Stanton was incensed that Black men received the right to vote before white women (488–94). The #MeToo movement of our time came to the forefront as a reaction and not a response to the Black Lives Matter movement.

Frederick Douglass and William Lloyd Garrison parted over ideological worldviews and priorities that involved Black suffrage and thinly veiled racism (183, 200–202). Whenever Black folks advance, there is a white backlash to that progress. White backlash or white supremacy has its antecedent. White supremacy lay at the taproot of Enlightenment movement.

14. Dorrien, *Breaking White Supremacy*, 83.

15. Immanuel Kant, quoted in Dorrien.

16. Renita J. Weems, "Reading Her Way through the Struggle: African American Women and the Bible," in *Stony the Road We Trod: African American Biblical Interpretation*, ed. Cain Hope Felder (Minneapolis: Augsburg, 1991), 57–80.

17. Martin Luther King Jr., *Why We Can't Wait* (New York: Signet Classics, 1963), xi–xii.

18. Eboni Marshall Turnman, *Toward a Womanist Ethic of Incarnation: Black Bodies, the Black Church, and the Council of Chalcedon* (New York: Palgrave Macmillan, 2013), 153.

19. Eddie Glaude Jr., *Democracy in Black: How Race Still Enslaves the American Soul* (New York: Broadway, 2016), 6.

20. W. E. B. Du Bois, "Jesus Christ in Texas," in Du Bois, *Darkwater: Voices from within the Veil* (New York: Harcourt, Brace, 1920), 70–77.

21. Henry Louis Gates Jr., *The Signifying Monkey: A Theory of African American Literary Criticism* (Oxford: Oxford University Press, 1988), 59.

22. James H. Cone, *The Cross and the Lynching Tree* (Maryknoll, NY: Orbis, 2011), 31–32.

23. See "How the Affordable Care Act Has Narrowed Racial and Ethnic Disparities in Access to Healthcare," The Commonwealth Fund, January 16, 2020, https://www.commonwealthfund.org/publications/2020/jan/how-ACA-narrowed-racial-ethnic-disparities-access.

24. West, *Cornel West Reader*, 279.

25. W. E. B. Du Bois, "Of Alexander Crummell," in *The Souls of Black Folk* (New York: Bantam Classics, 2005), 159.

26. Jean-François Lyotard, *The Postmodern Condition: A Report on Knowledge* (Minneapolis: University of Minnesota Press, 1984), xxiv.

27. Terry Eagleton, *Why Marx Was Right* (New Haven, CT: Yale University Press, 2018), 6.

28. Terry Eagleton, *Culture* (New Haven, CT: Yale University Press, 2016), 31–32.

29. Cornel West, *Race Matters* (New York: Vintage Books, 1994), 22–23, italics added.

30. Joseph Evans, *Lifting the Veil over Eurocentrism: The Du Boisian Hermeneutic of Double Consciousness* (Trenton, NJ: Africa World Press, 2014), 4.

31. King, "Pilgrimage to Nonviolence," 37–38.

32. Martin Luther King Jr., *Why We Can't Wait*, in *A Testament of Hope: The Essential Writings and Speeches of Martin Luther King Jr.*, ed. James M. Washington (New York: HarperOne, 1986), 524–25.

33. John R. Tyson, *School of Prophets: A Bicentennial History of Colgate Rochester Crozer Divinity School* (Valley Forge, PA: Judson, 2019), 80–81.

34. King, *Strength to Love*, 514.

35. Henry Louis Gates Jr., *Tradition and the Black Atlantic: Critical Theory in the African Diaspora* (New York: Basic Civitas Books, 2010), 118.

36. Pat Buchanan, quoted in Gates, *Tradition and the Black Atlantic*, 118.

37. Jean-Paul Sartre, *Being and Nothingness: The Principal Text of Modern Existentialism* (New York: Washington Square Press, 1984), 68–69.

38. F. F. Bruce, *New Testament History* (New York: Galilee Doubleday, 1969), 208–9.

39. John B. Pohill, *Acts*, New American Commentary 26 (Nashville: B&H, 1992), 64.

40. Henry Louis Gates Jr., *Loose Canons: Notes on the Culture Wars* (Oxford: Oxford University Press, 1992), 144.

41. Gates, *Loose Canons*, 116.

42. Herman Melville, quoted in Gates, *Loose Canons*, 116–17.

43. Evans, *Lifting the Veil over Eurocentrism*, 66. See also Gates, *Signifying Monkey*, 25; Chaim Perelman and L. Olbrechts-Tyteca, "Dormant Metaphors," in *The New Rhetoric: Treatise on Argumentation* (South Bend, IN: Notre Dame University Press, 1969), 404.

44. Martin Luther King Jr., "I Have a Dream," in *A Testament of Hope: The Essential Writings and Speeches of Martin Luther King Jr.*, ed. James M. Washington (New York: HarperOne, 1986), 217–18.

45. McFague, *Metaphorical Theology*, 138.

46. Paul Ricoeur, *Interpretation Theory: Discourse and the Surplus of Meaning* (Fort Worth: Texas Christian University Press, 1976), 45.

47. James H. Cone, *The Spirituals and the Blues* (Marynoll, NY: Orbis, 1972), 101.

48. Martin Luther King Jr., "Where We Are Going" in Where Do We Go From Here: Chaos or Community? (Boston: Beacon Press, 1968), 171–72.

49. Pohill, *Acts*, 27–28. Luke's Acts of the Holy Spirit was written as early as AD 57/59 to AD 150.

50. Martin Luther King Jr., quoted in Dorrien, *Breaking White Supremacy*, 301.

51. King, quoted in Dorrien.

CHAPTER 5

The Polished King Crafted Parabolic Sermons

> Now of course I was religious; I grew up in the church. I'm the son of a preacher, I'm the great-grandson of a preacher, and the great-great-grandson of a preacher. My father is a preacher, my grandfather was a preacher, my only brother is a preacher, my Daddy's brother is a preacher. So, I didn't have much choice, I guess. . . . But I had grown up in the church, and the church meant something real to me, but it was a kind of inherited religion and I had never felt . . . an experience with God in the way that you must have it if you're going to walk the lonely paths of this life. Everything was done, and if I had a problem, I could always call Daddy, my earthly father; things were solved.
> —Martin Luther King Jr.[1]

Martin Luther King Jr. was an authentic heir of the Black church social gospel tradition. The son of Martin Luther King Sr., the younger King was afforded privileges and advantages that others would covet. For example, he had proximity and access to many of the Black church's pulpit luminaries, such as Mordecai Johnson, Vernon Johns, and Benjamin Mays. King was close enough to hear them talk about what informed their theology and craft of homiletics and the political context from which they preached Jesus as hope, resistance, and liberation. Sociologists and theologians acknowledge that the formation of the Black church is not monolithic; nevertheless, they describe the Black church as a catalyst for the Black community's survival and resistance to imperial power:

> The Black Church has always stood as the *symbol* of freedom, even when the exigencies of the times made it a "Negro" Church. But it

> was never completely unanimous on the issue of whether it must not be the instrument of freedom—a dilemma which shadows it to this day. Perhaps it is enough that it has produced some of freedom's most celebrated leadership—Nat Turner, Henry McNeil Turner, Adam Clayton Powell, Jr., Martin Luther King, Jr., and Malcolm X, to name a handful.[2]

Of historical significance, the second excerpt focuses on Dr. W.E.B. Du Bois and others influence and shaping the formation of the Black Social Gospel movement.

> Like any tradition, the Black social gospel can be defined broadly or narrowly. . . . The Black gospel that led to King came mostly from the protest group aligned with [W. E. B.] Du Bois . . . plus a tiny Socialist plank. The full-fledged Black social gospel combined an emphasis on Black dignity and personhood with protest activism for racial justice, a comprehensive social justice agenda, an insistence that authentic Christian faith is incompatible with racial prejudice, an emphasis on the social ethical teaching of Jesus, and an acceptance of scholarship and social consciousness.[3]

King grew into understanding the culture of the Black church and community by learning to feel its experience and study its political and spiritual anatomy. If bodily surgery were necessary, a highly credentialed and skillful physician would be required—a person with a steady hand and a sharp scalpel to remove infectious connective tissue between the bones. It is plausible to see the church and community as extensions of each other, and King became such a physician. He grasped the complexity of Black culture's anatomy.

Firmly grounded in the Black church tradition, he developed an ear for its rhythms and cadences. In addition to its music's sweetness, Black preaching also has a sweet sound. We have heard that sweetness in a preacher's voice as poetic, as living metaphors. For the Black preacher, using living metaphors to dramatize preaching stories seems to be natural. Indeed, living metaphor underlies the best of Black parabolic sermons. This part of the craft is heard, mimicked, and developed early. It is an apprenticeship of the word of Divinity.

King was an apprentice of the Word, the Black tradition and culture, and its preaching. Those things seize upon Black preachers early in life:

> The child of the African American congregation grows up in the atmosphere of signals and effects that hums with authority of the performed word. The fledgling preacher's first teacher is, in fact, that atmosphere, which . . . a youngster absorbs by "osmosis." The first moment in the decision to preach is recognition of the power of the spoken word. . . . Plato was afraid of the orators because he knew that a properly constructed sequence of words has the inherent power of compelling assent. Aristotle did the first scientific study of speaking and concluded that the greatest thing by far is to be a master of metaphor, for such a master makes connections that others cannot make and thereby captures language for his own political [and preaching] ends.[4]

Over time the apprentice King became a master of the art of metaphor that is a prominent feature of the Black parabolic sermon by taking it beyond semantics and artifice. Not only did he understand the Black church's atmosphere, signals, and hums, but he also demonstrated repeatedly his ability to construct sequences of words. However, as mentioned above, Plato would have feared King's syntactical abilities and at the same time admired his inherent oratorical power over words. When King's living words are extended, we develop an appreciation for his parabolic sermons that parallel Aristotelian word pictures.

Like Aristotle, King powerfully deployed word pictures as extended metaphors. His art of metaphor helped congregants make sense of the sociopolitical, economic, and socio-human existential crisis. This seems to define the function and nature of a parable: "The numerous parables found in the Bible, and the paradigms of Plato and Platonistic writers, are not necessarily drawn from the realm of matter. They may be drawn from daily life in order to illuminate aspects of social, political, or moral life and to endow them with a particular structure of value."[5] King's parabolic sermons intentionally make visible hegemonic inequities. He revealed a divide between Black and white worlds and how their interpretations of realities differ.

Often parables are informed by models of allegory and are topical. The former is defined as symbols that point toward other symbols, and the latter is commonly referred to as topics, which is defined as placing an event, for example, alongside a more familiar one. This connects the unfamiliar event with the familiar one, and as a result, these are rhetorically considered as a common topic. The following definitions of allegory and topics or topical and how each shapes and functions as hermeneutic cues illustrate how we interpret parables. Hugh Blair, the first Regius Professor of Rhetoric and Belle Lettres at the University of Edinburgh,[6] writes,

> Allegory is a figure frequently found in them [parables]. When formerly treating this figure, I gave, for an instance of it, that remarkably fine and well supported Allegory, which occurs in the Eightieth Psalm, wherein the People of Israel are compared to a Vine. Of parables, which form a species of Allegory, the Prophetical Writing are full: and if to us they sometimes appear obscure, we must remember that in those early times, it was universally the mode throughout all the eastern nations, to convey sacred truths under mysterious figures and representations.[7]

About topical, Lane Cooper says, "The common translation, 'topic' suggests a rubric or category, a general heading under which specific details are collected or things are said. To Aristotle . . . it is a live metaphor he thinks of a place in which the hunter will hunt his game."[8]

In King's preaching, he "used allegory for the same reason the church always used allegory: to permit a richness of expression not obtainable from historical literalism, which is another way of saying that he wanted to use the text in his own world."[9] In the African American tradition and in King's sermons,

> typology discerns . . . continuity between figures as they are repeated in the Bible and as they occur in history. . . . Typology is the most important form of figural interpretation, for it allows for the fullest

> participation of one reality in another. Allegory, which is the assignment of external values of textual figures, plays a less significant role in the same tradition. Both methods are employed in . . . rich and allusive reading [and preaching] of Scripture.[10]

Indeed, King makes good use of allegory and topic in his parabolic sermons. Before King, allegorical language was central to early church leaders' interpretation (hermeneutics) of Scripture.[11] Biblical texts for them point to symbolism and underneath those symbols. The goal is to locate and interpret deeper dimensions of meaning. Once deeper meaning is discovered, Black pulpiteers know how to make related contemporary topics intersect with ancient biblical characters and then make both ancient and contemporary characters and intersecting circumstances walk together around their church sanctuaries to have conversations with the faithful congregants.[12]

Throughout this book, I have focused on the various tools that advanced the polished King. I have made claims that his employment of living words is a part of how we understand his thought process. In short, tracing metaphor toward King, we are able to narrow our scope and take measure of his thought process that we ground in his metaphorical process. King developed a metaphorical process that includes his hermeneutic, narrative, rhetoric, theology, and homiletic. These support our claim and point us toward the polished King.

I cannot capture King's complete thought process in my assessment, but I confidently claim that I am approximate. His metaphorical process expressed in his oral and written words provides some light on his thinking. In this chapter, however, I am concerned with investigating an intersection between King's theology and homiletic and more narrowly how his living metaphor functions as a significant part of his parabolic theology and parabolic sermons.

Parables and Parabolic Theology

As mentioned, we see parables as extended metaphors that inform King's use of parables in his sermons.[13] Underneath his parabolic sermons, King's theology squarely points toward his Black social gospel orientation. Once again, I employ the illustration of a grapevine. King's theology and homiletic are nearly inseparable. I understand King's parabolic theology to be similar to what follows:

> A theology that takes its cues from the parables finds that the genres most closely associated with it are the poem, the novel, and the autobiography, since these genres manifest the ways metaphor operates in language, belief, and life. Hence they are prime resources for a theologian who is attempting an intermediary or parabolic theology—a theology that is, on the one hand, not itself parable and, on the other hand, not systematic theology, but a kind of theology which attempts to stay close to the parables.[14]

If we develop an appreciation for King's use of metaphor, we can take hold of its intersection between his theology and homiletic. King's homiletic is a part of his metaphorical process and complements the whole. His theology is not dogmatic and therefore provides flexibility and intellectual space to explore his biblical texts and look underneath in order to understand the intermediary meaning that is present in the parabolic tradition and sermons. I define intermediary meaning as deferred understanding of meaning. Deferred meaning attracts us to the nature of parables.[15]

In King's preaching of a biblical parable, I see deferred meaning, and I see Du Boisian pragmatism, or what I have elsewhere called the Du Boisian prophetic tradition.[16] A masterful example of Du Boisian living words comes from a eulogy about a great man:

> This is the story of a human heart, —the tale of a Black boy who many long years ago began to struggle with his life that he might know the world and know himself. Three temptations he met on those dark dunes that lay gray and dismal before the wonder-eyes of the child: the temptation of Hate, that stood out against the red dawn; the temptation of Despair, that darkened noonday; and the temptation of Doubt, that ever steals along with twilight. Above all you must hear of the vales he crossed, —the Valley of Humiliation and the Valley of the Shadow of Death.[17]

This is also a brilliant example of effective use of a metaphorical process. The example helps us to recognize straightaway a word picture that we must interpret to move forward. This word picture introduces an exceptionally gifted boy who represents every young and gifted Black person's body and mind. Emphasis is placed on the Black mind and not the Negro mind. By Negro mind, I mean a representation of a person who has not come to terms with her or his double consciousness. Double consciousness in this context is narrowly defined. It refers to the mindset of persons who do not feel they can think and live freely as Divinity has gifted them without consequences for their self-actualization, actions, or decisions.

The writer has crafted a parabolic text that points toward liberation. As the narrative continues, we take notice of the boy's physical and psychological boundaries, one of which is limitations placed on his self-actualization. This is an extended metaphor that underscores the willingness of a dominant culture to deprive others of their opportunities to act on their natural and intellectual curiosities that lead to social and spiritual maturity. This is not democratic. It is undemocratic because it thwarts human progress, in this instance, Black socioeconomic and sociopsychological progress. Moreover, it is undemocratic to deny people's personhood.

Take notice, the Black boy faces what seem to be cosmically induced temptations. The writer describes dominating cultural vanguards who have strategically created and designed demonic webs to entrap, frustrate, and defer Black advancement. This alone is enough to prevent people from fulfilling their destiny and completing their journey. The writer describes a boy who would dream and achieve as "the wondrous-eyed child." The writer then makes us aware that the wondrous-eyed child, who represents the oppressed, faces vales of humiliation and the shadow of death (Psalm 23:1-4). This is a brilliant eulogy that I characterize as a parabolic eulogy; additionally, it points toward a parabolic theology. Theology alongside a preacher's homiletic shapes the form of sermonic development.

Parables appear frequently in the gospel. Parables add to the understanding of the original hearers (and now readers). Parables make us aware that often universally we share similar human experiences. The parabolic tradition is pedestrian, something that occurs in our neighborhoods, on our streets, and inside our homes:

The Polished King Crafted Parabolic Sermons

> The parable is a prime genre of Scripture and certainly the central form of Jesus's teaching. Current scholarship sees the parable as an extended metaphor, that is, a story of ordinary people and events which is the context for envisaging and understanding the strange and the extraordinary. In the parabolic tradition people are not asked to be "religious" or taken out of the world; rather, the transcendent comes to ordinary reality and disrupts it. The parable sees "religious" matters in "secular" terms. Another way to put this is to speak of Jesus as the parable of God; here we see the distinctive way the transcendent touches the worldly—only in and through and under ordinary life.[18]

Through parables we recognize our worst and best choices, behaviors, sins, and paths toward redemption. Some may see parables as ethical stories that teach people how to recognize the unethical and at the same time how to embrace the ethical. Parables point toward moral and ethical principles. I add, King's employment of parables parallels the traits of ethical pragmatism that we have located in the Black social gospel. Like Jesus of Nazareth, King crafted his parabolic sermons to uncover the presence and power of Divinity in the earthly realm. In so many words, King used parables to point us toward Divinity's transcendence. But what is underneath the parable?

Beneath the parable's story line is pathology. All brilliant narratives have brilliant story lines and characters. Where there are brilliant stories, there are patterns of human behavior, which is pathology. What follow are two biblical parables that are examples of narrative and story line and the pathology that lay underneath: "The kingdom of heaven is like treasure hidden in a field, which a man found and covered up. Then in his joy he goes and sells all that he has and buys that field. Again, the kingdom of heaven is like a merchant in search of fine pearls, who, on finding one pearl of great value, went and sold all that he had and bought it" (Matthew 13:44-46, ESV).

The two parables are related and intersect. Both are used to discern the indiscernible, that is, the kingdom of heaven. The writer employs a simile: "the kingdom of heaven is like." This is metaphorical language, and therefore it is not an exact description of heaven. However, it is a word picture that attracts us to the possibility.

It is significant that parables are rooted in our human condition. For example, people want to find treasures and pearls. Our discovery, we believe, indeed may bring substantial relief to our socioeconomic pressures. In context, Jesus' original followers were socio-oppressed people. In our global context, many people are struggling to survive economically in a world that has plenteous resources. In our contemporary context, our resources are not equally distributed and shared among the undernourished and underfed global masses. Moreover, we live in a time of uncertainty about the present and beyond. Many people have unclear and contradictory thoughts about heaven and more broadly about the possibilities of a painless and burden-free existence after death. However, most people hope to experience redemption and eternal life.

In addition, biblical parables point toward what people value and hold in common. The parables are powerful in large part because each is told assuming that its hearers have preunderstanding and predispositions that make parables culturally interesting. The parable is attractive and piques our curiosity if not our understanding.

For example, we can presuppose that all people would like to discover a treasure hidden in the field or a rare pearl. In most places in the world, these material objects are considered to be valuable. Each can be traded on an open market and exchanged for monetary value. However, beneath the surface of the parables, we can locate our common pathology. Often people have mistakenly thought that possessing monetary wealth ensures its possessors an impregnable fortress along with admired security and status. I concede that there is a level of security and status afforded to people who have financial resources. I contend, however, that Jesus points out that by comparison, entering the kingdom of heaven is certain status and security and more valuable than earthly wares that cause worries and woes.

Thus, in this instance, the parables about the hidden treasure in the field and the rare pearl are about comparing worldly wares with eternal life. The parables are thus interpreted to point people toward choosing between the world's temporal treasures and the eternal treasures of heaven. Underneath the parables' story lines there is an ethical corrective and alternative to our dysfunctional pathologies. In short, parables are adroit, sophisticated, moral, and ethical motifs. It is the hidden nature and purpose of the parables that attract us.

After discovering the treasure, the first prospector makes plans to sell his worldly goods to purchase the field where the treasure had been hidden. In the second parable, the searcher sells all personal goods to purchase the single pearl. He must have made a strategic plan to shrewdly sell all his personal goods. It is that pearl's quality that makes it more valuable than all of the searcher's worldly possessions. After peeling the outer layers from the parables, underneath we see the chain stich. The value of the kingdom of heaven is greater than the value of worldly possessions.

Underneath the parables, we discover unexamined evidence. Once the value of the kingdom of heaven is understood, its value causes radical behavioral changes. In the parables of the hidden treasure in the field and the rare pearl, the prospector and the searcher sell all their possessions. The parables offer the original and contemporary hearers and readers a counterintuitive story line that is an alternative to story lines of our world order.

Those who have found the value of the kingdom of heaven invest in it. Why? Because there is a practical aspect to selling all that we have to become citizens of heaven. The person who finds hidden treasure in a field is persuaded there may be additional treasure hidden there, and therefore shrewdly purchases the field. In short, people who discover the kingdom of heaven will take unlimited and radical risks to possess it. The parables are crafted to persuade people to heed Jesus' teachings, and his message is clear: it is in our best interest to invest in the kingdom of heaven. These parables, then, are models of ethical behavior and making radical choices.

Parabolic Theology in the Sermons of Thurman and King

King searched underneath the surface of parables to discover paradoxical and practical truths. In so doing, he helped his audiences discover the fault lines deep in the recesses of their minds and hearts. What is more, through the power of the parables' story lines, King persuaded people to radically change their public and private behaviors and challenged them to make the best ethical choices. Thus, King's preaching was grounded in the Black social gospel tradition, which is a species of ethical pragmatism. King's parabolic theology and homiletic then intersect with those of Howard Thurman.

Thurman influenced the polished King. Throughout his ministry, King read Thurman's work. Thurman later advised King during the tumultuous years of the Montgomery boycott. King had considered pastoring a church that Thurman once served. As readers will see, King borrowed from Thurman's quotes and other theological underpinnings over the ensuing years:

> [King] considered taking over at Fellowship Church. He pored over Thurman's books, especially *Jesus and the Disinherited* and *Footprints of a Dream*. In his early ministry King quoted or borrowed from Thurman numerous times, notably in his sermons "A Religion of Doing," "Overcoming an Inferiority Complex" and "Living Under Tensions of Modern Life." After King broke through in Montgomery, Thurman advised him behind the scenes, usually about self-care of leadership. On the road, campaigning to break white supremacy, King carried a copy of *Jesus and the Disinherited.* American Christianity has no greater legacy than what King got from Thurman and [Benjamin] Mays.[19]

Thurman's influence on King is evident throughout the mentee King's career. I will briefly compare their styles and substance located in their parabolic theology and homiletic.

No doubt there are similarities between King's and Howard Thurman's parabolic theology and homiletic. Thurman's theology and homiletic, like that of King, were informed by Black social gospel (and theology).[20] Thurman is remembered as a brilliant scholar-preacher who delivered parabolic sermons powerfully and incisively; his sermons focused on the socio-human and socio-ethical mandates in New Testament parables. Scholars have taken careful notice of his parabolic sermons: Thurman's sermons challenge listeners, in large part because he stresses urgent responses and spiritual truths that lay hidden underneath a parable's thick layers.[21]

Thurman, in these sermons, insisted that individuals must take responsibility for their lives and for expressing compassion in community. The welfare of persons and thats of community are inextricably linked. Choosing to attend to one while neglecting the other is not only folly, but it fails to prepare for God's coming realm.[22] Thurman was a master of uncovering ethical choices that lay hidden beneath the surface of parables. He deployed parabolic theology intended to expose ethical choices to listeners and readers. Often his sermons began with meditations that served as supporting themes. In "Concerning Prayer: Prayer and Pressure," Thurman's meditation has a stanza that includes an intercessory prayer: "Hold them, O peace of God, until Thy perfect work is in them fulfilled."[23]

We now set out to investigate Thurman's and King's parabolic theology and sermons. We begin with Thurman's "The Unjust Judge and the Friend at Midnight" (Luke 11:5-8; 18:1-5) and King's "A Knock at Midnight" (Luke 11:5-6). Second, we investigate Thurman's "Possessions" (Luke 12:13-21) and King's "Why Jesus Called a Man a Fool" (Luke 12:16-21).

Howard Thurman: "The Unjust Judge and the Friend at Midnight"

In "The Unjust Judge and the Friend at Midnight," Thurman's sermon introduction is protracted, pedestrian, and earthy. Thurman argued through his propositional statement that people pray often to achieve some material end. For Thurman, this is human selfishness. In our prayers, Thurman claimed, "we call [Divinity's] attention to ourselves, and our needs, and our desperation. We even enlist the support of other people that may become an organized pressure group, to wrest from the recalcitrant hands of an arbitrary God that which [God] is withholding."[24]

Thurman made a transition from his lengthy introduction, which included his sermon proposition, to his biblical texts. We call this a homiletic leap. He cited "two stories from the lips of Jesus [which] have been used again in this connection."[25] When preachers use multiple texts, it usually indicates the sermon's rhetorical strategy is informed by a topological narrative:

> One is a story of a judge who had no fear of man, no fear of God, no fear of fear. Apparently appointed for life, he was above the political process. A certain widow needed something desperately, something the judge could give her. Every time he came to his outer chamber, there she was. When he would start home for his lunch, she walked a respectful distance behind him, stating her case. Everywhere he went, there she turned up, always saying the same thing. "Will you do this for me?" And finally, he relented and did

> it, not because of any far-flung or intimate interpretation of the meaning of justice to which he was committed as a jurist. No. He did what the woman asked just because she kept worrying him, annoying him, harassing him; in order that he might have peace, he gave her peace.[26]

This parable teaches that prayer requires persistence. This may be a traditional interpretation and conventional on our part. Thurman, however, saw more; he read and interpreted the text against his hearing and interrogated the passage differently. Thurman was suspicious of Eurocentric hermeneutic claims.[27] What we call persistence, Thurman called pressure. In this way, a different word picture emerges: "Everywhere he went, there she turned up, always saying the same thing. 'Will you do this for me?'" Thurman then challenged listeners to acknowledge that there is a thin line between persistence and pressure. "Pressure should not be put upon God. The right place for pressure is upon me, upon you, to bring my life, your life, in its totality, to an exposure to God."[28]

There is merit in Thurman's hermeneutical and theological approach. It represents a foreshadowing path that points to "otherwise" people's hermeneutics, theology, and homiletic. Here I define otherwise people's hermeneutic as an African American invention:

> African American people or "otherwise people" comprise a well-chronicled example of how a different textual interpretation can become a model for forming a different hermeneutic that will influence pulpit speech for decades to come. People of color have learned to interpret what non-people of color think of them and alongside what people of color think of themselves. This, in brief, is Du Boisian double consciousness, the hermeneutic of otherwise people.[29]

This statement is consistent with Thurman's worldview. Thurman perceived that those canonical texts belong to the world's interpretation, and therefore canonical texts require a multifocal lens. Thurman was aware of globally organized socio-marginalization and oppression. What is more, we see an intersection between Thurman's hermeneutic and what is now commonly referred to as postmodern and poststructural hermeneutics, narrative, rhetoric, theology, and homiletics, or what I have attached to King and now to Thurman, a metaphorical process.

I contend that postmodernity and poststructuralism are traced toward species of Black philosophical and theological constructs. By this I mean the Black social gospel theology and movement. Others have come to this conclusion, and still others suggest that Thurman's work has inspired others to protest and resist hegemonic practices and demand that action be taken toward their liberation:

> *A postmodern and postindustrial American postscript:* Although Thurman's message of the 1940s was focused on the needs of Black representatives of the disinherited in the United States, by the last half of the final decade of the twentieth century, it was clear that his message was now replete with significance for many other people as well. Latinos, Native Americans, Southeast Asians, and many women and gay and lesbian people were only the most obvious additions to Thurman's community of the wall. For the pressures of postindustrialist capitalist world order had pushed many other people against a great variety of unfamiliar and unexpected walls (and glass ceilings), and we were hounded by the inner demons of fear, hypocrisy, and hatred. Thus, Thurman had to be taken seriously when he still offered this word "for those who need[ed] profound succor and strength to enable them to live in the present with dignity and creativity."[30]

Thurman's message is attractive. It brings attention to Black social gospel liberation motifs associated with African American resistance to hegemonic practices. This includes Eurocentric hermeneutics and theology. From a social location of white privilege, these are conceived and constructed.

In a similar fashion, Thurman told a second story that is informed by another parable. I have an appreciation for Thurman's reading against the conventional understanding of the text. Informed by Thurman, I posit there is a thin line between persistence and pressure:

> The other story is that of a man who had unexpected visitors late one night. They were overnight visitors, and hungry. He didn't have any food to give them. Jesus says he didn't have any bread. But he remembered his neighbor next door might have some bread that he could borrow. He knocked at the door, and the neighbor asked, "Who is it?" He identified himself, saying, "I didn't come for a social call; I want to borrow some bread."
>
> "But I can't get up; I don't know if I have any food; besides, I was just getting off to sleep after wrestling with insomnia for a long time [this does not appear in the biblical text]. Now you come to disturb me. Go on back home like a good neighbor." He drifted off to sleep, but the knocking came again; he was called back into consciousness. On and on that went, until finally he got up. He gave bread to his neighbor, not because he loved him, not because he cared anything about the hungry visitors. He gave the bread finally because he wanted to go to sleep. Now the picture that comes to us is that God is like that, that God has to be convinced, that he can be convinced only if we give him no ease, until at last we bend his will to meet our private demands. Pressure! Pressure! Pressure! . . . I think this says something about God that is unworthy; terribly unworthy! The point of the stories is not as is often indicated that God must be subjected to pressure in order to act on our behalf.[31]

Thurman affirmed my view that reading and interpreting parables involves discovering what is underneath the surface. Beyond the surface, there is a deeper and thicker layer of understanding that is to be considered in order to interpret parables. For a parable's "story is 'thick,' not transparent; like painting, it is looked at, not through."[32] Thurman's parabolic sermon is used to redefine pressure beyond persistence and reintroduces pressure as human selfishness.

Thurman deployed his parables to point toward his listeners' common perspective and behaviors. When human needs are perceived, many people participate in individual and group prayers. These prayers, according to Thurman, are a reactionary response that emerges as pressure and desperation. Thurman made this claim early in his sermon: "We call [Divinity's] attention to ourselves, and our needs, and our desperation." He brilliantly added, "The meaning [of prayer]? I respond to pressure of human need with such utterness that I cannot separate myself from the need. Therefore, I can never lay bare my own soul to the life, to the love, to the scrutiny, to the wisdom, to the judgment of God, without including in it others' needs that keep pulling at me."[33]

If we align with conventional interpretations of Luke 11:5-8 and 18:1-5, we grasp that the texts signify persistence. If we consider that Thurman's interpretation of the same texts underscores pressure, we are able to accept their plausibility. Why? Because we accept that Thurman's employment of parables points to paradoxical meaning and truth claims. A second reason is that a parable's meaning is open-ended. Thus, there is more than one strain of meaning that can surface simultaneously from the text of a parable.

Notice that I did not mention allegory in Thurman's first sermon. He did not employ this rhetorical tool; however, his sermon is replete with topical commonplaces. Nevertheless, his readers are surprised with a new awareness of paradoxical meaning; our persistence can be acts of desperation and pressure.

Still, we see Thurman's employment of living words as providing listeners with plausible meaning. Because of Thurman, we understand that our truth claims are approximate or references to reality. Last, Thurman's theology and homiletic intersect, too, and appear nearly inseparable. I suggest this intersection is like our example of the grapevine. At its intersection, it forms a circle. The circle represents a species of theological ethics that we ground in the Black social gospel tradition.

Martin Luther King Jr.: "A Knock at Midnight"

We now turn to the mentee King. We will notice that his sermon "A Knock at Midnight" (Luke 11:5-6) parallels Thurman's sermon "The Unjust Judge and the Friend at Midnight" (Luke 11:5-8; 18:1-5). King's sermon introduction is topical—many effective sermons begin with a historical or current event. This creates a similar word picture that provides a common frame of reference for listeners. King considered the parable to be a living metaphor for persistence in prayer, even calling persistence powerful: "Although this parable is concerned with the power of persistent prayer, it may also serve as a basis for our thought concerning many contemporary problems and the role of the church in grappling with them. It is midnight in the parable; it is also midnight in our world, and the darkness is so deep that we can hardly see which way to turn."[34]

He continued,

> It is midnight within the social order. On the international horizon nations are engaged in a colossal and bitter contest for supremacy. Two world wars have been fought within a generation, and the clouds of another war are dangerously low. Man [Human Kind] now has atomic and nuclear weapons that could within seconds completely destroy major cities of the world. Yet the arms race continues and nuclear tests still explode in the atmosphere, with the grim prospect that the very air we breathe will be poisoned by radioactive fallout. Will these circumstances and weapons bring the annihilation of the human race?[35]

King began his introduction dryly. However, his rich baritone voice dramatized his living words, and they stuck. As mentioned, King interpreted the parable as a call to persistent prayer. For King, this provided a sermonic point of departure for his audience.

King suggested that an open-ended parable can be reinterpreted and relocated plausibly and applied as a defining guidepost for the role of the contemporary church. He posited that the church's role is to grapple with contemporary problems. Furthermore, King framed his audience's expectations by doubling the extended metaphor. The parable's meaning, according to King, can be applied to contemporary political and economic systems. King demonstrated this; his listeners gained a new awareness. It is "midnight in our world, and the darkness is so deep we can hardly see which way to turn." King pointed toward nihilism (see chapter 4), which continues to affect us.

Nihilism is consistent with King's melancholy tone about the dismal plight that is stamped upon much of Black America. One thoughtful scholar links nihilism with America's hegemonic structures. If the structures do not cause Black folks' nightmares, certainly the structures hinder Black folks' dreams:

> The most basic issue now facing Black America: *the nihilistic threat to its very existence*. The threat is not simply a matter of relative economic deprivation and political powerlessness—though economic well-being and political clout are requisites for meaningful Black progress. It is primarily a question of speaking to the profound sense of psychological depression, personal worthlessness, and social despair so widespread in Black America.[36]

The prophet King's use of the parable demonstrated the parable's prophetic function. The knock at midnight in our world is nihilistic. We look to Eurocentric, globalized wars. These wars are equal to globalized terrorism for people of color both internationally and nationally. Domestically, police brutality, for example, is offensive and destructive politically and an economically sanctioned act that represents terrorism for Blacks, browns, and other marginalized people groups. War and conflict further compromise democratic progress for people of color economically and politically. King wanted to liberalize access to higher education, fair housing, and adequate health care. White supremacy inhibits these possibilities and results in hopelessness and lovelessness. "We can hardly see which way to turn" is nihilism. I suggest then that King utilized his allegorical model to interpret the parable's symbols. The symbols point to and signify that America and the world are in a time of bleakness and a period of uncertainty.

King made a second hermeneutical leap. He interpreted the parable as "midnight in our social order." His living words characterize a global existential threat. Again, King's focus was centered on a globalized existential threat that appears on the surface of the body politic. However, beneath the surface is philosophical and theological nihilism. King went further and said that nihilism is nothing less than a "colossal and bitter contest for [white] supremacy." In this way, we grasp that the two world wars that King mentioned are racialized wars, and these are wars over ideologies.

To this point, American empire has benefited from the two world wars. The winner of the wars has been empowered to continue Eurocentric dominance and hegemonic practices. We must not forget that the fascist beliefs in Italy and Germany were and are European constructs. King's "knock at midnight" includes the environmental crisis. Atomic and nuclear energies are used as weapons of war. The victims of weapons of mass destruction are not limited to time, place, and human faces; instead, irreversible damage is done to our ecological systems. Weapons of mass destruction leave irreversible toxins in the air we breathe. The melancholy King was prophetic about our destructive and contemporary hegemonic culture.

As we consider the body of King's parabolic sermon, we notice that King, unlike Thurman, shifted into allegorical language. Because parables by nature are open-ended, King saw rhetorical space to expand the symbolism of the parable. Parabolic symbolism, as I have suggested, points toward multiple layers of meaning. King accepted this assertion. Like Thurman, he continued to look underneath the parable's surface to find new awareness that is approximate to his and our contemporary settings:

> It is also midnight within our moral order. At midnight colors lose their distinctiveness and become a sullen gray. Moral principles have lost their distinctiveness. For modern man [and woman], absolute right and wrong are relative to likes and dislikes and the customs of a particular community. We have unconsciously applied Einstein's theory of relativity, which properly described the physical universe, to the moral and ethical realm. . . .
>
> Midnight is the hour when men [and women] desperately seek to obey the eleventh commandment, "Thou shalt not get caught." According to the ethic of midnight, the cardinal sin is to be caught and cardinal virtue is to get by. It is all right to lie, but one must lie with real finesse. It is all right to steal, if one is dignified that, if caught, the charge becomes embezzlement, not robbery. . . .
>
> As in the parable, so in our world today the deep darkness of midnight is interrupted by the sound of a knock. On the door of the church millions of people knock. In this country the roll of church members is longer than before. More than one hundred and fifteen million people are at least paper members of some church or synagogue. This represents an increase of 100 percent since 1929, although the population has increased by only 31 percent.[37]

King continued to employ the living metaphor "midnight" as a signifier of dysfunctional domestic and international social orders. From this context, King's Black social gospel theology emerged, developed, and matured. He painted a word picture that expresses society's breakdown and lack of moral clarity. "At midnight colors lose their distinctiveness and become a sullen gray" is used here as an illustration that supports King's propositional argument, "Moral principles have lost their distinctiveness." King believed there are moral absolutes that are neither passive nor indifferent to fluid contemporary variants.

King declared that Einstein's theory of relativity became more than scientific theory; it became a popular and confused cultural trend mistaken for ethics. The discourse in the preceding paragraphs serves as a sample of how King used allegorical language. He used it to persuade listeners that indifference to moral and ethical "oughtness and shouldness" does not stop the knock at midnight. In fact, social indifferences, immoralities, and unethical behaviors are the cause for the knock at midnight. The knock interrupts the "sullen gray" status quo. In short, Divinity's presence disturbs our human indifference to human pain and suffering.

The knock at midnight, then, is a living metaphor that represents the presence and power of Divinity. For humanity, the knock represents Divinity's expectations. Divinity demands that action be taken and that we acknowledge that our world is hurting from unmitigated predatory economic systems. Thus far these systems are left nearly undisturbed, unreformed, and untransformed. These are some of the reasons that answer questions for why our nihilistic nightmare continues.

Howard Thurman: "Possessions"

Thurman's second parabolic sermon under our consideration is titled "Possessions." The introduction is a brief exposition of the parable of the rich man (Luke 12:13-21). He told his listeners that Jesus here communicated a simple and straightforward story. Thurman started, "The picture is carefully and skillfully etched: A man . . . is doing well . . . his farm has produced many things more than he can handle and dispose of."[38] Thurman then continued to describe the parable's movement and actions.

After introducing his listeners to the main character, a rich man, Thurman emphasized the purpose of the parable: to expose the rich man's motives—

"I will make room for them [possessions]."[39] Thurman added this satirical comment: "which is a very sound way to do it, I suppose."[40] Then he returned to the rich man's soliloquy: "I will make room so that I may store all of these things."[41] Thurman continued, "And very dramatically Jesus says the man's a fool because that night he dies."[42]

Thurman brilliantly presented the parable to his audience in a few precise words. He avoided confusion and unnecessary flowery words that would be considered gangling and inappropriate. He gained the trust of his audience and then could move into the body of his sermon.

Recall that Thurman's sermon title is "Possessions." After his effective introduction, Thurman addressed uncontrolled human obsession with material things. He then proceeded to ask his audience rhetorical questions strategically designed to cause his listeners to consider their motives for possessing things:

> If you measured your life in terms of units of concentration that could be transposed in terms of values, what would they look like? Let's not hurry over that. What would they look like? Take your day; take your week. Let's think about ourselves now. Take your week. How much of your energy, time during the past seven days, have you spent involved in things in which you believe? Or has your time been spent getting things out of the way so that you can have ten minutes to breathe? Or, are you spending your energy and your time working on behalf of those things? What about it? Or do you say to me: "If I had all of my other problems solved, then, of course, it would be a reasonable thing to assume that I could give my mind and thought over to these luxuries of the spirit or luxuries of the mind." Is that the way you feel? That so much of your energy and time must be spent guaranteeing your protection against either one or the other or both of these impersonal forces about which I spoke a moment ago. And therefore it is not a reasonable thing to assume that you can give your time and thought to something else. What about it? . . .
>
> Now the second question: How much detachment do you practice with reference to the things that encumber your life? How much

> of you do you put at the disposal of trying to work out the problem of your involvement? What is your fundamental attitude toward money, for instance? Is it an instrumentality by which you communicate and make active your will to dominate and control your fellows? This is a perfectly good question to ask. Now you can do that, you see, not merely if you are a person of great and vast economic power.[43]

Thurman skillfully outlined what he wanted his audience to consider. He intended for us to grapple with our motives and how our motives either subtract from or add to the quality of individual and collective human life. Thurman is focused overall on the community.

In his sermon body, Thurman was probing beneath the parable's symbols. He thoroughly investigated what we value. He asked his listeners to think about their lives and their values simultaneously to determine motive. Indeed, what we value points directly to how we spend our time, our money, and other resources, and how our actions affect human welfare. Our actions determine what and who we value. In short, Thurman was penetrating his audience's collective psyche to examine how we spend our time. "Or has your time been spent getting things out of the way so that you can have ten minutes to breathe?" Thurman wanted to know, are we responsible stewards over our time?

Second, Thurman wanted his audience to examine their motives as they relate to moral and ethical choices. This is the primary focus of Jesus' parable; the rich man was called a fool because he did not manage his assets well, and neither did he manage his resources to address human suffering. I add that the rich man was a fool because he was immoral and unethical. This lies at the symbolism and meaning of the parable. Jesus called the man a fool precisely for these reasons.

> How are you related to your money? How are you related to it? And it is no answer to say that you don't have any. That's no answer. How are you related to your money? Is it a part of your commitment to yourself? That's the crucial question. If I give all of my life goods to support causes in which I do not believe, or if I with-

> hold the bowels of my generosity and compassion from the need that always hammers at my door, then I will never find freedom of mind, of spirit, of heart. . . .
>
> Do I give my money, my things? Am I so attached to them that to detach myself from them is equivalent to destroying [me]? Or is it possible for me to put at the disposal of [others] the fruits of my labor, bearing in mind that everything that I have, I have because of a lot of other people's work, a lot of other people's sacrifice, a lot of other people's self-denial? It's the most stupid thing in the world for a man to say, "I did this myself." I didn't. . . . What about it? Are you willing to try it? See what happens.[44]

After he thoroughly investigated the parable, Thurman became a master investigator of the inner person. He looked beneath the surface of the parable to discover its symbolism. Once he had decided the parable's approximate meaning, without compromising its intention, he placed it inside contemporary culture. Thurman made "possessions" our ancient and contemporary foe.

Martin Luther King Jr.: "Why Jesus Called a Rich Man a Fool"

Like Thurman, King preached from Luke 12:13-21. King titled his parabolic sermon "Why Jesus Called a Rich Man a Fool." As mentioned, Thurman focused on the inner person to unearth our inward motivations. In short, Thurman posited, what people value indicates how people value human lives. This is a clear indication of what Divinity expects. That is, Divinity declares that it is our moral and ethical obligation to aid the oppressed. If we see this and refuse, we have failed to understand that our stewardship responsibilities are indeed moral and ethical mandates.

In this way, King's approach was similar. King understood the parable as a symbol that points toward stewardship and responsibilities thereof. Like Thurman, King affirmed Divinity's expectations for wealthy people. That is, wealthy people are to recognize Divinity's mysterious grace, and their resources are bestowed on them to support the basic human needs of the oppressed. Like Thurman, King probed underneath the surface, but King's interpretation provided him rhetorical space to reframe and relocate the parable's symbols and meaning into his contemporary world. In this way, King discovered space to speak prophetically and politically about current conditions. We will briefly examine King's introduction and parts of his sermon body. Then we will look at some of the subtle nuances that support King's surprising conclusion to his sermon.

King's sermon introduction is deliberately long and protracted. He addressed many topics, including his credibility with his congregation:

> I did not come to Mount Pisgah to give a civil rights address; I have to do a lot of that; I have to make numerous civil rights speeches. But before I was a civil rights leader, I was a preacher of the gospel. This is my first calling and it still remains my greatest commitment. . . . I have no other ambition in life but to achieve excellence in Christian ministry. I don't plan to run for political office. I don't plan to do anything but remain a preacher.[45]

All could hear King's heartfelt motivation. He affirmed that his calling was to serve as a preacher in Christian ministry. He gave every indication that he knew that he was in a safe space. That is, he was in a Black church's sanctuary, in a Black church pulpit, where there was liberty and expectation to preach the gospel. For the invitation, King voiced his personal appreciation and satisfaction. He knew it was a privilege to deliver the worship service sermon. Nevertheless, we sense that the burdened King knew also that he was permitted to vent and brood openly. As did his original audience, we know that he carried a daily burden related to the civil rights struggle. His admission included an acknowledgment. He knew that he was a significant figure, but with that came unavoidable and overwhelming responsibilities.

King used his introduction to deploy his rhetorical strategy. First, he wanted to connect with the congregation. As mentioned, the congregation was familiar with the public King, but he reminded people that he was a pastor. He seemed to go out of his way to assure the assembly of his commitment to Christian faith and to the local church. King doubtless tried to connect emotionally. That is, the loving King sympathized with his audience and their human anxieties. At that time, King lived in Chicago and had witnessed some of the cruelest living conditions imposed and sanctioned by law upon Black people. The northern states, like the southern ones, reinforced white supremacy and hegemonic practices. King was empathetic with the congregation and their family members. They certainly must have appreciated his concern for their welfare. Also, by then most people would have understood that each time King preached, it could be his last time.

After his introduction, he made an adroit homiletic move toward the parable's narrative:

> I want to share with you a dramatic little story from the gospel as recorded by Saint Luke. It is a story of a man who by all standards of measurement would be considered a highly successful man. And yet Jesus called him a fool. If you read that parable, you will discover that the central character in the drama is a certain rich man. This man was so rich that his farm yielded tremendous crops. In fact, the crops were so great that he didn't know what to do. It occurred to him that he had only one alternative, and that was to build some new and bigger barns so he could store all of his crops. And then as he thought about this, he said, "Then I'm going to do something after I build my new and bigger barns." He said, "I'm going to store my goods and my fruit there, and then I am going to say to my soul, 'Soul, thou hast much goods, laid up for many years. Take thine ease, eat, drink and be merry.'" That brother thought that was the end of life. . . .
>
> But the parable doesn't end with that man making his statement. It ends by saying that God said to him, "Thou fool. Not next year, not next week, not tomorrow, but this night, thy soul is required of thee."[46]

King recited the parable. He painted pictures that further explain the extended metaphor. King dramatized the Epicurean's attitude: "Take thine ease, eat, drink, and be merry." Epicureanism is an example of nihilism. There is an emptiness that underscores the pursuit of material happiness at the expense of experiencing the broader gift of human life.

Three times King mentioned the human soul: "I am going to say to my soul, 'Soul, thou hast much goods.'" The third time, King emphasized that Divinity has required "thy soul." His approach differed from Thurman's approach to this parable. The parable for King highlights that personal income and wealth are not as valuable as the human soul. In fact, because Epicurean pursuits are deceptive, many do miss this simple point; nothing we possess is more valuable than our souls. And when a nation becomes Epicurean, nihilism takes root in the body politic and culture. For King, this was his America, and yes—it is our America now.

Further into the sermon body, King's reinterpretation and relocation of the parable highlight the parable's transcendent and universal meaning:

> I'd like for you to look at this parable with me and try to decipher the real reason that Jesus called this man a fool. Number one, Jesus called this man a fool because he allowed the means by which he lived to outdistance the ends for which he lived. You see, each of us lives in two realms, the within and the without. Now, the within of our lives is that realm of spiritual ends expressed in art, literature, religion and morality. The without of lives is that complex of devices, of mechanisms and instrumentalities by means of which we live. The house we live in—that's part of the means by which we live. The car we drive, the clothes we wear, the money that we are able to accumulate—in short, the physical stuff that's necessary for us to exist. Now the problem is that we must always keep a line of demarcation between the two. The rich man was a fool because he didn't do that. . . .
>
> Somehow in life we must know that we must seek first the kingdom of God, and then all of those other things—clothes, houses, cars—will be added unto us [Matthew 6:33]. But the problem is all too many people fail to put first things first. They don't keep a sharp line of demarcation between the things of life and the ends of life.[47]

King understood traditional and conventional interpretations of the parable. We see his Thurman-like concern for the inner person. He further understood that the approximate meaning of the parable is revealed by its underlying symbols and that those symbols point toward a web of symbols. In this way, King provided for himself rhetorical space to reinterpret the parable's symbols and relocate its multilayered meaning in his contemporary context. In addition to the inner person, the parable addresses the outer person. For King, the parable pointed toward the whole person. It was not an either-or but a both-and proposition.

We see how King intersected his theology with his homiletic. King envisioned that the parable makes us aware of the emergent kingdom of God in the earthly realm. The presence and power of Divinity take precedence over human priorities. The rich man who is called a fool, then, is representative of all people who have not placed their priorities alongside those of Divinity. In our pursuit of material things, we can be subject to and possessed by objects instead of becoming passionate about people and committed to deploying our resources to meet human needs. This is at the root of the kingdom of God:

> Now, number two, this man was a fool because he failed to realize his dependence on others. Now, if you read that parable in the book of Luke, you will discover that this man utters about sixty words. And do you know in sixty words he said "I" and "my" more than fifteen times? This was a fool because he said "I" and 'my" so much until he lost the capacity to say "we" and "our." He failed to realize that he couldn't do anything by himself. This man talked like he could build the barns himself, like he could till the soil himself. And he failed to realize that wealth is always a result of the commonwealth.[48]

We notice King's employment of allegorical language. With allegories, King transported the extended metaphor and relocated the selfish man and placed him inside our gone-awry American socioeconomic order. Philosophically and religiously, capitalism stresses individualism and not community. As well, our socioeconomic order and culture have psychological effects and influences on the nation's pathology and body politic.

This includes the occupants of the Oval Office and those on local school boards. Historically, both have been protectors and wards of the status quo. I characterize the status quo as blatant white supremacy and hegemonic practices. King's America and ours is fatally flawed and has failed to become aware of its avarices, failed to repent and take corrective actions to abolish all forms of human oppression. White supremacy is flawed and oppressive, and it is not of Divinity. By comparison, Divinity is concerned with human beings bringing forth human justice. By contrast, Divinity demands that human resources are shared with the oppressed populations. King expressed this claim—that is, Divinity is concerned with "the commonwealth," the emergent kingdom of God.[49] This is Black social gospel theology that emerges as an ethic.

Knowing the Presence and Power of Divinity

I began this chapter with a quotation chosen to help us frame our concerns with the intersection between King's Black social gospel theology and his homiletic. At the outset, I characterized King as an authentic heir of the Black church social gospel tradition, which includes "his afforded privileges and advantages that others would covet." Yet King found himself facing an existential crisis. In chapter 4, I referred to this self-disclosed event as King's kitchen-table experience. I think it may be better described as his Pentecost experience.

At his kitchen table, King came to know the presence and power of Divinity. Like King, we know that Divinity's presence, power, and calling to serve divine purposes are beyond conventional words. King began to close his parabolic sermon in so many words by adroitly explaining himself to be a parable inside of the (biblical) parable:

> Something said to me, you can't call on Daddy now; he's up in Atlanta, a hundred and seventy-five miles away. You can't even call on Mama now. You've got to call on that something in that person that our daddy used to tell you about. That power that can make a way out of no way. And I discovered then that religion had to become real to me and I had to know God for myself. And I bowed down over that cup of coffee—I never will forget it. And oh yes, I prayed a prayer and I prayed out loud that night. I said, "Lord, I'm down here trying to do what's right. . . . I'm losing my courage.

> And I can't let the people see me like this because if they see me weak and losing my courage, they will begin to get weak. . . ."
>
> And it seemed at that moment that I could hear an inner voice saying to me, "Martin Luther, stand up for righteousness, stand up for justice, stand up for truth. And lo, I will be with you, even until the end of the world."
>
> . . . And I'm going on in believing in him. You'd better know him, and know his name, and know how to call his name. . . .
>
> But sometimes you can get poetic about it if you know him. You begin to know that our brothers and sisters in distant days were right. Because they did know him as a rock in a weary land, as a shelter in the time of starving, as my water when I'm thirsty, and then my bread in a starving land. And then if you can't even say that, sometimes you may have to say, "He's [my] mother and father." If you believe it and know it, you never need walk in darkness.[50]

Thus, during his kitchen-table experience, King came to know Divinity intimately and personally. His prayer is considered confessional because he acknowledged his sense of discouragement and vulnerability. He had been released from the fear of failure. Ironically, this is liberation, for fear is another manifestation of materialism. Then the spiritual King claimed that Divinity's personality is uncovered as a moral and ethical agent. Divinity as an agent manifests as an advocate for justice. What is more, King's testimony is also a confession. He confessed that if he had not accepted his parents' experience and perception of Divinity, he would not have had a point of departure to grasp his new reality. His mother's and father's God had become his own. King was brilliant because he admitted that, however nuanced, however subtle, or adroit, he was the rich man whom Jesus called a fool. This is the autobiographical King because, within King's theology and his preaching of parables, there is biography that listeners can adapt and personalize.[51]

Up to this point, King had been seduced into believing that he, too, could engage in life on his own terms. King was perhaps unaware that he was making newer and larger barns. Barns represent here King's acquisition of forthcoming titles and positions, broader global recognition, and public acknowledgments and achievements. King's living words point toward prophetic insight that uniquely highlights that his living words are incarnational.

This is a superb example of King's theology and how it intersects with his homiletic. We have seen in this chapter that King's living words create union with his metaphorical process. Furthermore, his living words are recognizable to most people of faith in the African American religious tradition. What may not have been recognizable to audiences is that King's theology and homiletic are nearly inseparable. This remained consistent whether King was speaking on public platforms about civic issues, civil rights, and democratic concerns, or elsewhere. His theology and homiletic could be heard while he was answering probing questions from skillful television news interviewers. His theology and homiletic could also be heard in his rhetoric, that is, in how he organized his words and used them to persuade. King was consistently rooted in the democratic tradition, informed by his Black social gospel tradition.

It is in the pulpit, however, where King became the polished King! I assert that he is also the parable King. I return to my claim that King's living words are incarnational, and I add that King, too, is incarnational. For the parable is incarnational, and those who interpret, reinterpret, and relocate multiple layers of meaning into new contexts with new awareness are living parables of God. I understand that I am making both a theological and a political statement. But like all speech, theology is political. It serves as an insurgent agent into and against all hegemonic practices and the body politic. Jesus has been called the parable of God:

> Jesus as the parable of God did not tell people about the kingdom, but he was the kingdom; and the way his whole life brought people to the kingdom was through juxtaposition of the ordinary within a startling new context. If theology is to be parabolic, it must attend very closely to these features; that is, it must not be concerned primarily with explaining and systematizing concepts about the kingdom but must look carefully at the way parables function, both the ones in the New Testament and Jesus as a parable. For [Leander] Keck says, the goal of a parable is not "to impart concepts about the kingdom but to make it possible for men [and women] to respond

> to it." This, the possibility of response, is what we have called the task of theology. . . . It is a coming to a moment of insight [advent and emergence] when one's ordinary situation is seen in a new setting, a startling setting (called "the coming of the kingdom" in the New Testament). This moment of insight is not a discrete mystical moment, but, again, if we take our clues from the parables, one emerges from one's story and has implications for all of one's life.[52]

King is a parable of God (not *the* parable of God that we associate with Jesus of Nazareth, but *a* parable of God). King's life was also a life filled with juxtapositions. His Black social gospel theology became the most significant and consequential movement of the twentieth century. The juxtaposition is that it was informed by and a continuation of the Black social gospel movements that preceded his. King did not try to explain his movement as much as he modeled it. He did not live long enough to reflect on his journey, and therefore he was not afforded time and space to systematize his theology of the kingdom of God. His theology, then, remains parabolic, open-ended, and pliable for reinterpretation and relocation into the resistance of other socio-oppressed people. Some have tried to usurp King's living words and actions nefariously, but their efforts have fizzled because they were obviously pretentious and envious attempts to duplicate King's polish—to no lasting avail.

Those who understood the movement understood King. And sadly, there have been many who have not understood the movement and therefore failed to understand King. Joyfully, many people hear Divinity's voice through King's life and movement. Their response is to become catalysts for justice. Through action taken, the newly radicalized understand that Christianity is a movement and is not necessarily systematized. The Christian movement is a parable. King is a parable of God, an extended metaphor; a preacher possessed with incarnational living words that tell a story. His authentic Christian story is his personal story and our stories, and our stories like King's are living words.

Notes

1. Martin Luther King Jr., "Why Jesus Called a Man a Fool," sermon delivered at Mount Pisgah Missionary Baptist Church, Chicago, Illinois, August 27, 1967. See also Martin Luther King Jr., *A Knock at Midnight: Inspiration from the Great Sermons of Reverend Martin Luther*

King Jr., ed. Clayborne Carson and Peter Holloran (New York: Warner, 1998), 161–62.

2. E. Franklin Frazier and C. Eric Lincoln, *The Negro Church in America and the Black Church Since Frazier* (New York: Schocken, 1974), 108.

3. Gary Dorrien, *The New Abolition: W. E. B. Du Bois and the Black Social Gospel* (New Haven, CT: Yale University Press, 2015), 3.

4. Richard Lischer, *The Preacher King: Martin Luther King Jr. and the Word That Moved America* (Oxford: Oxford University Press, 1995), 39.

5. Chaim Perelman and L. Olbrechts-Tyteca, *The New Rhetoric: A Treatise on Argumentation* (Notre Dame, IN: Notre Dame University Press, 1969), 383.

6 Hugh Blair, *Lectures on* Rhetoric and Belle Lettres, ed., Linda Ferreira-Buckley and S. Michael Halloran (Carbondale: Southern Illinois University Press, 2005), xxxiii.

7. Blair, *Lectures on* Rhetoric and Belle Lettres, 473.

8. Lane Cooper, ed., *The Rhetoric of Aristotle* (London: Prentice-Hall, 1932), xxiv.

9. Lischer, *Preacher King*, 206.

10. Lischer, 202.

11. Lischer, 7, 199.

12. Lischer, 202–3.

13. Cleophus J. Larue, *The Heart of Black Preaching* (Louisville, KY: Westminster John Knox, 2000), 27–29.

14. Sallie McFague, *Speaking in Parables: Study in Metaphor and Theology* (Minneapolis: Fortress, 2007), 3.

15. Joseph Evans, *Lifting the Veil over Eurocentrism: The Du Boisian Hermeneutic of Double Consciousness* (Trenton, NJ: Africa World Press, 2014), 29. See also McFague, *Speaking in Parables*, 5.

16. Evans, *Lifting the Veil over Eurocentrism*, 10.

17. W. E. B. Du Bois, "Of Alexander Crummell," in *The Souls of Black Folk* (New York: Bantam, 1989), 159.

18. McFague, *Speaking in Parables*, 2–3.

19. Gary Dorrien, *Breaking White Supremacy: Martin Luther King Jr. and the Black Social Gospel* (New Haven, CT: Yale University Press, 2018), 171.

20. Dorrien, *Breaking White Supremacy*, 96–97.

21. David B. Gowler and Kipton E. Jensen, eds., *Howard Thurman: Sermons on Parables* (Maryknoll, NY: Orbis, 2018), xii.

22. Gowler and Jensen, xiii.

23. Gowler and Jensen, 146.

24. Gowler and Jensen, 147.

25. Gowler and Jensen, 147.

26. Gowler and Jensen, 148.

27. Paul Ricoeur, *Memory, History, Forgetting* (Chicago: University of Chicago, 2004), 295. See also Josiah Ulysses Young III, *A Pan-African Theology: Providence and Legacies of the Ancestors* (Trenton, NJ: Africa World Press, 1992), 15.

28. Gowler and Jensen, *Howard Thurman*, 150.

29. Evans, *Lifting the Veil over Eurocentrism*, 12. See also John McClure, *A Postmodern Ethic for Preaching* (St. Louis, MO: Chalice, 2001), ix.

30. From Vincent Harding's foreword to *Jesus and the Disinherited* by Howard Thurman (Boston: Beacon, 1996).

31. Gowler and Jensen, 150.
32. McFague, *Speaking in Parables*, 5.
33. Gowler and Jensen, *Howard Thurman*, 148–49.
34. Martin Luther King Jr., *A Knock at Midnight: Inspiration from the Great Sermons of Reverend Martin Luther King Jr.*, ed. Clayborne Carson and Peter Holloran (New York: Warner, 2000), 65.
35. King, *A Knock at* Midnight, 65–66.
36. Cornel West, *Race Matters* (New York: Vintage, 2001), 19–20, italics in original.
37. King, *A Knock at Midnight*, 67–68.
38. Gowler and Jensen, *Howard Thurman*, 71.
39. Gowler and Jensen, 71.
40. Gowler and Jensen, 71.
41. Gowler and Jensen, 71.
42. Gowler and Jensen, 71.
43. Gowler and Jensen, 75.
44. Gowler and Jensen, 75.
45. King, *A Knock at Midnight*, 146.
46. King, *A Knock at Midnight*, 147–48.
47. King, *A Knock at Midnight*, 149–50.
48. King, *A Knock at Midnight*, 151.
49. Martin Luther King Jr., "The World House," in *Where Do We Go from Here: Chaos or Community?* (Boston: Beacon, 1968), 177–202.
50. King, *A Knock at Midnight*, 161–63.
51. McFague, *Speaking in Parables*, 178.
52. McFague, 82–83.

Afterwords

I remember when the new books arrived. My parents had purchased the *Ebony Pictorial History of Black America*. It came in a three-volume set, and each book was wrapped in cellophane. I suppose the wrappers were meant to protect the books from moisture and possibly to prevent other kinds of damage. Each book's spine was exposed, and we gripped it to remove the books from the box. I can still see the books' brown covers, trimmed in gold letters. The pages were stiff, and therefore, I concluded, they had remained untouched until we opened our box set.

The books also came with a familiar antiseptic smell that I still associate with dreaded visits to our family physician, the gray-haired, tobacco-chewing Dr. Wolfe. However, that distinct smell added to my excitement and anticipation. I could not wait to see what the books were about. I suppose that special smell made me feel special too. By that time, I began to understand that our family did not have disposable income. We wasted nothing. Everything we had was used until its usefulness had expired. Thus, I knew we would not waste our means on frivolous things. The books would become a special family heirloom.

So, I sat quietly for hours reading the content of the volumes. From the brown books trimmed with gold letters, I learned more about African American culture, traditions, values, and contributions to our black community and the larger society than I did throughout my elementary and secondary educations combined. I suppose this was the primary reason the books were published. The Johnson family, publishers of both *Ebony* magazine and this box set, knew that black children and adults across the country were languishing and uninformed, which left us feeling bereft, and incapable of self-rule and self-determinism.

What added to the purpose for publishing these special books was African Americans' ongoing need to be made self-aware. It is black awareness that provides the courage and righteous indignation to fight and resist the hegemonic and supremacist propaganda that underscores white mythologies. So, because of the new books with the antiseptic smell, I gradually developed a new confidence and sense of identity. I learned not to believe what the white schoolteachers said about me because I knew something about myself that they did not. I began to know that, someday and in some way, I would walk in the Du Boisian prophetic tradition. The same tradition that informed Dr. Martin Luther King Jr.'s living words.

Once, while reading one of the volumes, I was startled by a particular photograph. In grainy black and white, it captured the polished King dressed in what appeared to be a tan-colored suit, white shirt, and striped black and white tie. Atop King's head was a white Fedora hat with a neat black satin band. The graphic photo was an image of the helpless King, who had been pushed into an uncomfortable and compromised position. His arms were forced behind his back, and his hands were trapped in handcuffs. King was made to appear, at least to me, like one of those criminals or gangsters I had seen in numerous movies on television.

I called to my mother. I needed an explanation and, I suppose, comfort. I could not understand why King was going to jail. The photo was taken in 1958 when he was arrested in Montgomery, Alabama, for a violation of local segregation laws. He was fined fourteen dollars but refused to pay, so he was sentenced to fourteen days in jail. At that time, in 1971, I knew nothing about King being an unlawful man. I knew he was a Baptist preacher. I knew his image was on our church walls, and also on the hand fans, provided by a local funeral home, that were behind our pew Bibles and Baptist hymnals in the pews' missalette boxes.

I knew that King's image was positioned in prominent spaces on the walls of every other church I had ever visited and, indeed, nearly everywhere in the black community. In our homes, his photograph was placed alongside a blonde-haired, blue-eyed image of Jesus. What I saw inside my new book was inconsistent with what I had been told—and taught. If King could be incarcerated, then every black boy I knew, good or bad, could and would be incarcerated.

My mother struggled to find the words to simplify what had happened to King. It was like what she said could happen to me. If I were believed to be a bad boy downtown, I could be arrested and go to jail. In fact, I am not sure her answer was adequate for a precocious ten-year-old boy. But now I know why King went to jail. He did so for justice—and for the sake of the gospel of Jesus of Nazareth.

I learned later that, on Good Friday in 1963, Dr. King and Ralph Abernathy were arrested, charged, and incarcerated for their peaceful protest against unjust segregation laws. The two men were leaders in the Birmingham bus boycott, demanding that action be taken against Jim and Jane Crow laws. Traditionally, on Good Friday many black churches are full of congregants attending worship services to affirm our faith and process our anguish that Jesus was lynched on a rugged cross, sanctioned by Roman law.

While black congregants in Birmingham affirmed their faith and purged their anguish on that Good Friday, King and Abernathy went to jail. Learning this helped me reach an understanding of how the cross and Jesus' thirst for righteousness intersects with the socio-human justice movement that King became a part of. And I have come to recognize, understand, and accept that I am part of the same movement. Therefore, *The Polished King* is my written contribution to that movement.

From the day I first saw that black-and-white photograph until now, I continue to be haunted. Each visit from the ghost of King in handcuffs has made me feel uncomfortable about our current and unresolved human condition. Writing this book has neither helped me escape those visitations nor removed the lingering antiseptic smell of those three brown books trimmed in gold letters. But engaging with King's living words helps me cope.

Index

E

F